The Education of Women
and *The Vices of Men*

Modern Intellectual and Political History of the Middle East
Mehrzad Boroujerdi, *Series Editor*

Other titles in Modern Intellectual and Political History of the Middle East

The Education of
WOMEN

TWO QAJAR TRACTS

&The Vices of
MEN

Translated from the Persian and with an Introduction by

HASAN JAVADI
and
WILLEM FLOOR

Syracuse University Press

First Complete English Edition 2010
10 11 12 13 14 15   6 5 4 3 2 1

Originally published in Persian as *Ruyaru'i-ye zan va mard dar 'asr-e Qajar. Du resaleh. Ta'dib al-Nesvan va Ma'ayeb al-Rejal,* eds. Hasan Javadi, Manzheh Mar'ashi, and Simin Shakarlu (San Jose, 1371/1992).

For a listing of books published and distributed by Syracuse University Press, visit our Web site at SyracuseUniversityPress.syr.edu.

ISBN: 978–0-8156–3240–5

Library of Congress Cataloging-in-Publication Data
Ta'dib al-nisvan. English
The education of women ; and, The vices of men : two Qajar tracts / translated from the Persian and with an introduction by Hasan Javadi and Willem Floor. — 1st complete English ed.
p. cm. — (Modern intellectual and political history of the Middle East)
Includes bibliographical references.
ISBN 978-0-8156-3240-5 (cloth : alk. paper)
1. Women—Iran—Social conditions—19th conditions. 2. Women—Sexual behavior—Iran. 3. Sex customs—Iran. 4. Wives—Iran—Conduct of life.
5. Husbands—Iran—Conduct of life. 6. Iran—Social life and customs—19th century. I. Javadi, Hasan. II. Floor, Willem M. III. Astarabadi, Bibi Khanum, b. 1858 or 9. Ma'ayib al-rijal. English. IV. Title. V. Title: Vices of men.
HQ29.T3413 2010
305.48'89155009034—dc22   2010031695

Contents

Illustrations

Introduction

The Debate on Women

In 1304/1886–87, a small booklet was published in Tehran by an anonymous author. It was entitled *Ta'dib al-Nesvan,* or *The Education of Women,* and it immediately caused a furor in that city.[1] The booklet made such an impact that very soon after its publication a French translation appeared.[2] What was the fuss about? In ten chapters, the anonymous author of *The Education of Women* not only wanted to educate women on how to behave properly toward their husbands, but also to put them in their place because he considered the women of the Tehran upper class rather uppity. Although the book is addressed to all women, it is clear that the author's main target was upper-class women, who had not only servants, but also a mind and will of their own. The female readers and listeners did not like the kind of education the author recommended for all women. Why did they not like it, considering that most of the rules were straight from traditional Islamic teachings? Like their male counterparts, many upper-class women of this time had been exposed to new, mostly European ideas about law, equality, and education, which led to the questioning of age-old accepted "truths" about the role of women, their relationship toward men, and their place in society in general. Most men were not prepared for such a development, even when it did not really amount to much in quantitative terms at that time. However, the anonymous author of *The Education of Women* clearly felt that the situation as far as women were concerned threatened to get out of hand if someone did not tell women what proper behavior toward their husbands should be. As such, the text was as much aimed at husbands as it was at their wives. In taking this approach, the author was rather blunt and condescending and based himself firmly on the strength of religious tenets and traditions; he relegated a woman's role to a mere extension of her husband's pleasure in all respects. Only then was she a "good" woman; only then might she attain paradise. His basic recommendations were:

1. A wife should not question anything, and whatever her husband says, she should do it, for obeying her husband is her duty.

2. A wife should show forbearance and not utter a word that might create discord.

3. A wife should never complain about her husband, even though she may have a hundred reasons to do so.

4. A wife should never sulk, however much hardship she has to endure, for she has to see the positive side and be patient.

5. A wife should not walk fast, should hold her head high, and should not bend her back, and her gait should be graceful.

6. A wife should sit at the table *(sofreh)* on her two knees, while smiling, and should not chatter.

7. Nothing is more unattractive in a woman than to make use of animal fat for her head, face, and hands.

8. A woman should always wear clean clothes, and she should not show herself to her husband in dirty, greasy, and old clothes.

9. There is no room for prudishness and shame in bed.

10. In the morning, a wife should leave her husband alone; she should make herself beautiful for him and then come to him with a smiling face like a flaunting pheasant and a shining moon.

Although Tehran society at that time, whether Persian or European, did its utmost to establish the author's identity, nobody so far has succeeded in doing so. This secrecy is quite remarkable for a society where secrets were public goods. Therefore, people have been guessing who might be the author of these inflammatory words. Because of the booklet's somewhat amusing tone, it is not impossible that the author was a clever literate who wanted to poke fun at women's early efforts to propound their rights. However, given that the content of the message is a regurgitation of traditional Islamic views concerning the role of women, it may well be that the author was a conservative who dreaded the development of a trend that implied greater liberty and education for women. It has also been suggested that the author, whether a conservative or a satiric inciter, may have been wedded to a princess and that he was thus afraid of her retaliation if she ever found out he wrote this booklet. What seems to be clear, however, is that the author's mother tongue was not Persian, but Azeri Turkish. This conclusion is suggested by the author's phraseology, which often seems very much a translation from Azeri rather than normal Persian, and this impression is further reinforced by his frequent use of Azeri maxims.

Such a putting down of women demanded a reply, of course, and it came soon. Bibi Khanom Astarabadi wrote this reply in 1312/1894–95, and she called her rejoinder *Ma'ayeb al-rejal,* or *The Vices of Men.* From the introduction to her essay, it is clear that she had not intended to write

The Vices of Men, but women friends who had read and discussed *The Education of Women* urged her to do so. This
piece of information is interesting in itself because it shows
not only that women talked about more than their hairdos,
their clothes, and the like, but also that Bibi Khanom must
have been well known in these women's circles as somebody
with strong feelings about the matter of women's rights and
as somebody who had the literary skills to write a credible
and convincing critique.

Her rejoinder, which was not published until 1992, 102
years after its conception, is divided into roughly four parts.
After a short introduction, in "Advice to Women with the
Help of God" she provides a critique of each of the ten issues
raised by the anonymous author of *The Education of Women.*
In the third part, "The Vices of Men," she details the various
vices of men and asks her readers to judge whether women can
be good wives if their husbands behave in such a despicable
manner. And then in the fourth part she gives a short account
of her own life and marital troubles.

Bibi Khanom replies directly to each of the ten criticisms
in *The Education of Women.* First, she points out that many
men take advantage of their wives, squander their wealth,
and then move on to another wife to start all over again.
How can one respect such a man? Second, she points out
that because women are forced to lead a cloistered life, burdened with children and housework, they cannot do much
else, but nevertheless they are acquiescent. Third, Bibi writes
that if men behaved the same way toward their wives after the
marriage ceremony as they had before it, women would not
complain. Fourth, she argues that sulking is not a failing, for

if husband and wife love one another, sulking will engender affection, not dislike. As to the sixth complaint, that women should walk daintily and talk softly like a sick person, Bibi Khanom submits that such behavior might be possible for women who have nothing better to do. She reminds the author that in the real world women have a household to run. The seventh complaint, that women are not clean or scented, Bibi Khanom counters with the argument that this problem is caused by poverty. Men should just love their wives rather than boys, she adds. As to the eighth complaint, that women should dress according to their husbands' wishes, she counters that men often have no taste and that when women dress themselves with material bought with their own money, men generally show no interest at all in matters of clothing. In response to the ninth complaint, about sleeping habits, Bibi Khanom argues that this problem also stems from poverty and that living conditions force people to sleep together. Also, she reproaches the author for projecting his own sexual preferences onto all men, which she denies is true. Finally, as to the tenth point, that women should rise from bed before their husbands, Bibi Khanom submits that the entire argument is an excuse for the master to play with the servants while the wife is gone from the room.

In the third part of her essay, Bibi Khanom attacks men in general by listing their vices, which are focused on their own pleasure and lead them to ignore the needs of their wives and families. In four vignettes, she depicts men as alcoholics, gamblers, drug addicts, and debauchees. These descriptions are followed by a scathing diatribe about the nature of men's behavior toward their wives, regarding whom they only find fault and to whom they never offer a loving word of appreciation. She ends this part by pointing out that Naser al-Din Shah treats all women of whatever background courteously and that men should take him as an example.

Bibi Khanom concludes her book with a short description of her life, how she fell in love and married, how she and her husband had a conflict over a temporary wife, and how they finally reconciled.

Although both authors follow the florid style of the time and their Persian is heavily larded with learned words, appropriate quotations from the Koran or famous poets, and their own poetic products as well as sexually explicit language, Bibi Khanom ingeniously mixes her language with street Persian and slang words, and she includes popular ditties and stories that are bawdy and daring. Using the everyday language of the common people or slang expressions was something unprecedented in Persian literature, and its wider use did not start until the Constitutional Revolution. 'Ali Akbar Dehkhoda in his revolutionary days created a sensation by his famous essays *Charand Parand* (Chiavari) in the journal *Sur Israfil*. He further delineated his superbly inimitable style by using common expressions and slang words in his poetry. Some poets followed suit, among them Ashraf Gilani (Nasim-e Shomal), who translated the poems of the famous Azeri journal *Molla Naser al-Din* into Persian. But it was not until 1341/1923 that Jamalzadeh started a new and realistic style of prose in his "Yeki Bud Yeki Nabud" (Once upon a Time), which was the first modern short story in Persian. Bibi Khanom's use of slang words, common expressions, and bawdy language can be taken as one of the earliest examples of this new style. She is amazingly familiar with the expressions that Persian men used in their homosexual, gambling, drinking, and other intimate circles. She uses these terminologies so appropriately that some critics have said she must have been helped by a male friend.

Sexually explicit language has posed problems of translation for both texts. For example, G. Audibert, who translated *The Education of Women* into French in the late nineteenth century, chose not to translate all the explicit sexual language of the text but instead produced a bowdlerized version that was more acceptable to society at that time. He was followed in this approach by E. Powys Mathers, who translated Audibert's French text into English in 1345/1927.[3] In addition, Audibert and by extension Mathers did not make a literal translation of the text but rather rendered the content and spirit of the text into French and English, respectively. This approach resulted in a somewhat shorter text, and some of the "poems" in the translated text are in fact versified lines that occur in prose in the original Persian text. Nevertheless, the translations by Audibert and Mathers reflect the purports of the Persian original quite well, and that is what counts.

In translating *The Education of Women* and *The Vices of Men,* we decided, however, to produce faithful renderings of the Persian texts, without sacrificing readability, in order to give readers a better understanding of the language and phraseology used. Doing so was sometimes difficult because obscure or unknown rhyming slang words are not easily rendered in equally rhyming English. We have not expurgated the bawdy parts from our translation, as Audibert and Mathers did.

We have tried to keep the notes to a minimum so as not to overwhelm the reader with too much information that might dwarf the translated text itself.

Who Was Bibi Khanom?

The name of the author of *The Vices of Men* was known for some time, but not who she was. This lack of information was in part owing to the fact that her essay lay in the Majles Library gathering dust for one hundred years and was not published until 1992.[4] Since then, it has been published a second time.[5] Furthermore, some of Bibi Khanom's descendants came forward and made public their recollections of their mother and grandmother.[6] From these various published sources—in particular family recollections—it has been possible to sketch the life and accomplishments of Bibi Khanom, author of *The Vices of Men*.

Bibi Khanom Astarabadi was the daughter of Mohammad Baqer Khan Shir-kosh, the commander of the Astarabad cavalry, and Khadijeh Khanom, daughter of Akhund Molla Kazem Mazandarani. Her mother worked for thirty years as the teacher *(molla-baji)* of Shokuh al-Saltaneh, one of the wives of Naser al-Din Shah (r. 1264–1313/1848–96) and mother of Mozaffar al-Din Shah (r. 1313–25/1896–1907). According to Bibi Khanom, her mother was a good and generous person who had only two sets of clothes. Whenever one was washed, she gave it away and sewed herself a new one. Of her wages, she kept only what she needed for her own upkeep, and the rest she would give away as alms to the poor. Bibi Khanom's mother also did not insist on a large dowry for her daughter, so the amount actually received was low, and its payment was on credit. In addition, she helped her son-in-law financially during the first years of the marriage. Khadijeh Khanom died shortly before 1308/1890, the year that her namesake, Bibi Khanom's youngest daughter, was born.

Bibi Khanom's father, Mohammad Baqer Khan, was the chief of the Anzan District in the province of Mazandaran— a district consisting of eighteen subdistricts. According to Khadijeh Afzal Vaziri, Bibi Khanom's youngest daughter, Mohammad Baqer Khan allegedly made a name for himself when he killed a lion that attacked Naser al-Din Shah during one of the shah's visits to that province. Henceforth, he was known as the "lion killer." However, according to Bibi Khanom, the sobriquet *lion killer* had in fact been given to her grandfather, Karbala'i Baqer Khan, in the days of Fath 'Ali Shah after he cleft a lion into two parts with one cut of his sword. It was also he, rather than his son, who was given the office of chief of protocol of the royal court *(ishik aghasi-bashi)*.[7] During a visit to Tehran, Mohammad Baqer Khan became enamored of Khadijeh Khanom, and because she lived in the royal harem, he asked the shah for permission to marry her. After the marriage, he took her to Mazandaran, where she gave birth to Bibi Khanom in 1274 (1858–59) and Hoseyn 'Ali, who later became one of Mozaffar al-Din Shah's physicians. Bibi Khanom mentions that she had a sister, although we get no information about this sister from Bibi Khanom's daughter, Khadijeh Afzal Vaziri. Khadijeh Khanom was not very happy with her life in Mazandaran because Mohammad Baqer had five other wives, with whom he had five sons and five daughters. Also, life in Nowkandeh, the main village in her husband's lands, was not very comfortable for a woman who was accustomed to life in the royal harem.[8] Of the two servant girls she had taken with her, one died, and she herself also fell ill.

Khadijeh Khanom had a brother in Tehran, Aqa Sheikh Asadollah, who was a learned *mojtahed* (a high-ranking religious scholar). Undoubtedly at her urging, he came to Mazandaran and asked Mohammad Baqer permission to take his sister on pilgrimage to Karbala. Mohammad Baqer could not refuse, of course, and thus Khadijeh and her children left. When she returned to Iran, she went straight to Tehran, where she resumed her employment as a teacher *(molla-baji)* and never left the royal court again. Two years later Mohammad Baqer Khan was killed in his bed by an unknown enemy. His oldest son, Mohammad 'Ali Khan, upon whom the shah also bestowed the rank of *sarhang* (colonel), succeeded him in his functions. The latter's only son, Aqa Bozorg Khan, would later marry Khadijeh Afzal Khanom, Bibi Khanom's youngest daughter.

Thus, Bibi Khanom was raised in the royal harem, which explains her frequent visits there when she was married. She was a precocious child who was in the habit of scribbling on the walls. When Naser al-Din Shah asked who was doing that and was told "Bibi," he gave orders that she join the girls in the harem for education. While in Tehran, she fell in love with Musa Khan Vazirov (later renamed Vaziri), a tall, handsome young émigré from the Caucasus. According to Bibi's daughter, her grandmother was opposed to the marriage, so Bibi eloped and married Musa Khan when she was twenty-three years old and he nineteen. If this story is true, an elopement would be a unique occurrence for somebody of Bibi Khanom's class; it not only would have challenged the very core of patriarchal society, but also would have brought shame on the family. According to Bibi Khanom herself, however, it was her maternal uncle who opposed the marriage, and it was only because of her mother's support that she finally, after a four-year wait, was allowed to marry her beloved.

By that time, Musa Khan was an officer in the newly created Cossack brigade (1300/1882), where he reached the second-highest military rank, *mir-panj*. In addition to military duties, he, given his excellent mastery of Persian (his mother tongue was Azeri Turkish), also taught Persian in the Cossack brigade. Musa Khan was of a very friendly disposition and pleasant with his children, which earned him the nickname "Musa the Prophet" among his friends. He also allowed Bibi Khanom to rule his roost, the more so because she did not exceed proper womanly boundaries. Also, Musa Khan was a reformist who believed in equal rights for men and women, according to his daughter. He is said to have written a book about the lascivious lifestyle at the court of Naser al-Din Shah. Musa Khan Vaziri died in 1340/1922, one year after his wife, Bibi Khanom.

The marriage seems to have been a happy one, although with the usual ups and downs. As both Bibi Khanom and her daughter relate, in 1312/1894, when Bibi was thirty-six years old, Musa Khan took a temporary wife named Banu, with whom he had a daughter, Maryam Khanom Vaziri. Needless to say, Bibi Khanom was hurt by her husband's behavior, which led to their separation, although they later made up again, as she relates at the end of her book. It was after this unfortunate and traumatic event that she wrote *The Vices of Men* and that her youngest son was born.

From Bibi Khanom's marriage with Musa Khan, seven children were born: Mowlud, 'Ali Naqi, Fath 'Ali, Hasan 'Ali, Khadijeh Afzal, 'Ali Reza, and 'Ali Asghar. There was another child who died and whose name was given to Khadijeh. Because Bibi Khanom had grown up in the royal harem, many of her playmates had married and borne children there, so she was often invited to the royal harem and took her children with her. These contacts were useful for her children's later careers.

The three oldest boys were at first taught at home by a tutor *(molla-bashi)*. When Khadijeh Khanom was six, she was allowed to join as well. After the Kamaliyeh boys' school opened, Bibi Khanom sent her three oldest boys there. Khadijeh felt left out, so Bibi Khanom wrote to the head of the school asking that Khadijeh also be allowed to attend, albeit in boy's clothes and with a boy's name, to which the headmaster agreed. This disguise worked fine for a few days, but her brothers made the mistake of calling her "Moluk" (a name given to her by Mozaffar al-Din Shah) instead of "Mirza 'Ali Asghar Khan," her boy's name. She had to leave school and resume home schooling with her oldest sister.

Apart from Bibi Khanom's own accomplishments, her maternal uncle was a *mojtahed,* and the son of her maternal aunt was the chief calligrapher *(khosh-nevis bashi)* of the royal court, who would be succeeded by his son in that function when he died. Contacts with all these and other knowledgeable persons left their mark on Bibi Khanom and her children. They benefited from their learned relatives, who not only visited but also corrected the children's "homework." Khadijeh, for example, received writing lessons from the chief calligrapher himself. When they had filled their glazed drawing paper, they would wash it in the pond because the ink was washable and start anew when the paper had dried. Each night during wintertime, when the Vaziri children were sitting around the charcoal brazier *(korsi)* with parents, siblings, and cousins, they would read from a varied selection of books, and the adults present would correct mistakes immediately. Anybody in the family who knew anything came to Bibi's house and taught all her children, from how to play musical instruments to writing and arithmetic, for she believed that boys and girls should have the same education.

In 1324/1906, when Musa Khan held the rank of general *(sartip)*, he was appointed to command the Fars army. He left for Shiraz and took his two oldest sons with him. Bibi Khanom remained behind with the other children in their twelve-room house. It was then that she decided to begin a girls' school, which, apart from a few foreign schools, did not yet exist in Iran. Mirza Hasan Roshdiyeh had made an attempt to establish an Iranian girls' school in 1321/1903, but owing to opposition by religious groups he had been forced to close it after four days. Bibi Khanom's decision, therefore, was a brave one, for even when more girls' schools were opened later, opposition from reactionary groups remained intense. Stones were thrown at her school's billboard, and the pupils, mostly minors, were called whores and their school a brothel.[9]

In the new School for Girls, Bibi Khanom taught and was helped first by her oldest daughter, Mowlud Khanom, and later by her youngest daughter, Khadijeh Afzal. However, she had no experience in running a school and had no idea how to equip a classroom. She therefore imitated the classroom methods of the Cossack brigade school to which her oldest sons had gone; one of her sons, Hasan 'Ali Khan, told his fourteen-year-old sister, Khadijeh Afzal, how to arrange the classroom furniture, how to install necessary equipment in the rooms, and how to put a big map on the wall. Bibi Khanom was not yet satisfied, though, because her daughters had no experience in teaching. She therefore sent them to the American school to learn how to teach. At that school, they were taught the following subjects: English, geography, arithmetic—all in English. Meanwhile, Bibi Khanom obtained a permit to open the school. The new school had three classes, with twenty pupils in all, each class taught respectively by Bibi Khanom, Mowlud Khanom, and Khadijeh Khanom.

The establishment of the girls' school was such an astonishing event that it drew even the attention of foreign diplomats. In a letter to the British foreign secretary Sir Edward Grey, the British minister in Tehran, Sir Charles Marling, reported that his Russian counterpart, M. de Harting, had told him that a well-educated woman, a situation exceptional for somebody of her sex, three months ago had established a girls' school in Tehran, where girls of very good families were educated.[10]

During the bombardment of the Parliament (Majles) in June 1908, one of the reactionary clergy condemned the establishment of the girls' school. In a broadsheet, Sayyed 'Ali Shushtari, one of the conservative ulema living in Bibi Khanom's own quarter, declared her to be an infidel. Meanwhile, the rowdies of the quarter were preparing to attack and destroy the school. Bibi Khanom therefore was forced to close her school. She did not give up, however, and went to see the minister of education, Mokhber al-Saltaneh, to ask what she had done wrong and what he could do to help her. The minister said that he could not do anything against the clergy, but he advised her to change the school to one that taught four- to six-year-olds and to let the older girls go because Sayyed 'Ali Shushtari opposed only the education of older girls. So Bibi Khanom reopened her school and did as advised because she had no choice, although the older girls cried because they wanted to learn. She told these girls to come back later, when things quieted down. She also wrote an encouraging letter to

ADVERTISEMENT

The School for Girls

⁂

A new school, named "The School for Girls,"
has been opened near the old Mohammadiyeh
gate of the Hajji Mohammad Hoseyn market.

THIS SCHOOL consists of a large courtyard and numerous rooms equipped with all necessary school requirements.

For the opening of this school five female teachers have been appointed, each responsible for one subject, such as Nakhost-nameh [elementary reading], Writing, History of Iran, Reading, Cookery book, Law, Religion, Geography, Arithmetic. Teaching will be adapted to the learning ability of each girl or woman.

In addition, a room has been set aside for teaching in manual arts, such as knitting, gold embroidery, silk embroidery, sewing, etc. All these teachers are women and with the exception of an aged porter, no other man will be in the School.

Pupils between the ages of seven and twelve will be accepted. The cost for the elementary class is fifteen and for the advanced class twenty-five qerans per month. Discount is offered to those in reduced circumstances. For every two pupils [from the same family] one will be accepted free of charge. It is hoped that thousands of schools such as this one are to be opened in our dear motherland.

Signature: Bibi [Khanom Astarabadi].

(Published in the Majles daily newspaper of 9 Safar 1325/28 March 1907.

1. Advertisement for Bibi Khanom Astarabadi's School for Girls. *Majles,* 9 Safar, 1325/28 Mar., 1907.

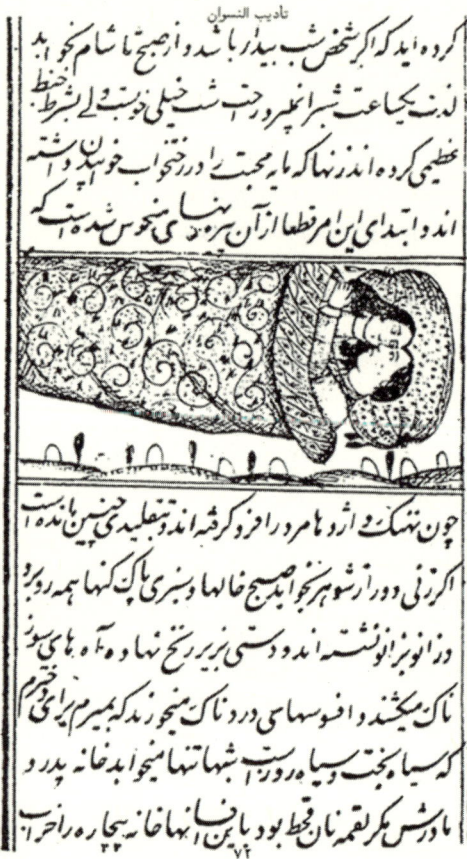

2. A page from the lithograph edition of *The Education of Women*. N. N., *Ta'dib al-Nesvan* (Tehran: n.p., 1304/1886–87).

the deputies besieged in the Majles building and sent her head scarf with it, stating, "Be steadfast in defending the Constitution or put on my head scarf." The letter was read aloud in Parliament.

Meanwhile, the school continued its work unhindered for a year. In 1909, when Musa Khan was transferred back to Tehran, Bibi Khanom's quiet house became a busy one again. Her husband insisted that she now discontinue the school; she refused and instead rented a house nearby and conducted the school there, now even receiving older women (forty-seven to sixty years old) as pupils. Bibi Khanom also started to teach embroidery, sewing, cooking, and confectionary because she considered them necessary womanly requirements. In 1329/1911, when she felt tired and too old, she closed the school. Her oldest daughter, Mowlud Khanom, then established her own girls' school, where her sister Khadijeh Afzal Khanom was one of the teachers while she continued her studies and obtained her teacher's certificate. Like her mother, Khadijeh Afzal Khanom wrote letters to various newspapers and journals promoting women's rights.

Not only were Bibi Khanom's daughters accomplished persons, but her sons also did well. Colonel 'Ali Naqi Vaziri, her oldest son, was a musicologist, composer, celebrated player of the *tar*, and the founder of both the Academy of Music of Iran and Iran's National Orchestra. As a result of his accomplishments, he became known as the father of modern Persian music. He may have inherited his musical talent from his mother, who also sang and played the drum *(zarb)*. Hasan 'Ali Vaziri was a pupil of Kamal al-Molk, Iran's most celebrated painter, and became a well-known painter himself.[11]

PART ONE

The Education of Women

Foreword

[After praise of God and the Prophet, the author states:] A friend of mine who was an intimate confidant and a solace to my woes said: "When I was young and the down on my face was just sprouting forth, when the tree of youth was adorned with the fruits of desire, and the time of youth was freshened by the breeze of spring, and my tender face had not yet been wrinkled by life's vicissitudes, and my youthful condition had not yet suffered from life's trials,

> The hue of my cheek was red like a Judas-tree
> The fortune of youth was smiling upon me.

"Not more than eighteen years of my life had passed when in accordance with the custom of that time I asked the hand of one of my relatives in marriage, and so at the beginning of youth I was afflicted with the hardships of wife and children. Eleven years of my dear life were wasted until she died because she did not have a good temper, which is a requirement of womanhood. Despite all this, our love was mutual, and thus for a year I was consumed by grief on account of her death, and I vowed that I would not marry again and take a permanent wife from a distinguished family. I thought that I was the only man who had to cope with a shrewish wife and that no one else had suffered from the same problem. But I did not know that humankind is the same and that this affliction is common to all, except women."

In this valley wasting away alone I am not
Because of you, many hands like mine are raised to God.[1]

Fortunately, one day when I was talking to a friend about such a subject, we discussed the behavior of women. I said, "I believe that no one before me has suffered like me on this account." He looked at me in a friendly fashion and smiled. I asked him why he smiled. He gave me a few pages that an important person had written about his life so that whenever I am sad, I should read them. I still have those pages. Because this author also was afflicted with the problem [of women], I begged to have his thoughts on the subject and took those pages, and after reading them, I took my pen and made some changes in those pages. I divided them into ten chapters. If this little book pleases the gracious gentlemen, I will be extremely fortunate, and I hope that they will give it to their daughters so that they will read it in the schools. And if they are not pleased with it, I hope that they will not criticize the lady of the house. Apologies are always accepted by the best of men.

Preface

Concerning Little Girls Who Have Been Spoilt by
Their Parents and Will Not Make It in Any Society

The reason [girls are spoiled] is that from the beginning of life until puberty they eat nothing but delicious dishes, drink cold beverages, and hear nothing but "Little Lady." Every nurse says, "My little lady, the moon cannot compare with you in beauty," and [the girl] imagines herself to be as fair as a peacock of paradise. The parents, as the saying goes, stuff her ears with vapid compliments such as, "Oh my dear pretty one, may I be your sacrifice, do not accept a suitor because he has a turban or the other one that wears a large mantle[2] or a third one who does not have a proper head of hair. Your husband must be like a king, not like this poor beggar." She has heard such nonsense from the beginning of her life until the moment that she leaves for her husband's house, and thus her head is filled with it. In effect, thanks to the credulity of the weaker sex, they believe such talk, and when she goes to the house of the husband, she makes her own life and that of the husband darker than my life.

Then a crowd of old women gather around her, heaving sighs that such and such a girl is unfortunate and that her husband does not appreciate her. They do not understand that man has been created to experience suffering and hardship so that as long as he lives, he will waste his precious life and earn worldly possession for the sake of his wife, children, and family. In fact, one who has no relations and does not care for anything has gained nothing either from this world or from the world to come. And, in fact, he finds no joy in both worlds.[3] However, the beginning of difficulties and the suffering of hardship is getting married and having children, which is the cause of many sorrows in this and the next world, and the poet has well said:

> O thou who art burdened with a family,
> Think no more of ever enjoying tranquility.[4]

Yet without wife, children, and worldly possessions, you cannot prosper in this or the next world.

Among the greatest difficulties of the world is marriage, and this relationship has often caused men to leave their mother, father, brother, and other relatives and to throw themselves into great dangers and live their life in perpetual hardship. Therefore, the matter of marriage is of great importance, and God the Merciful has decreed this affair. Thus, man has no choice but to marry. Those who have abandoned this world either have denied God's decree or were ignorant of this world. Nevertheless, real men have suffered under this burden, but they had no choice but to exercise forbearance and patience. Don't you see that as soon as a woman is married to a man whom she has not seen before in her life and never has even heard his name, she becomes so attached to him that she leaves all her relatives and family? In the whole world, she has chosen you, and for the sake of the love for her husband she does not begrudge him her wealth and even her life. She will do anything to gain his affection. If she sees a deceitful charlatan, she loses her money through deceit and fraud by buying such things as a paper scribbled in red ink that, God forgive me, has been diluted with donkey's fat and has been offered to her as a talisman of love. She will believe this donkey skin to be Tartary musk and dried cow dung to be powdered perfume. She seeks the aid of a hyena's genitals, which, in the trade, is the most desired means of getting love, so that she can gain the affection of the husband.

> Love has done many such things and will do so again
> It has turned a Sufi's robe into that of a monk like a refrain.[5]

She is unaware that all these things are nonsense and that magic cannot affect anything and will not bring any affection. But their hunger is never sated. Pillow talk is needed, not the genitals of hyenas. Charming manners are required, not exquisite fabrics; wood is for burning, not for gaining love; unclean skins should be thrown away, they are not a means for gaining affection. Love comes from charming behavior, not from ugliness or beauty. The essence of love is good manners, silence, propriety, and charming conversation.

> These points are sharp as diamonds
> If you don't have a shield, flee the field
> Don't face this sword without a shield
> Since it does nothing but cut to make points.[6]

Beauty constitutes only one part out of one hundred; if beauty is accompanied with sharp temper, then there is no doubt that ugliness would be better. There is no animal more colorful and beautiful than a snake, but because of its poison we flee at its sight.

> Not everyone with a total shave of hair is a friar
> Not everyone who makes a mirror is an Alexander.[7]

Not everyone sternly enthroned with hat askance
Knows the art of justice and governance.[8]

An engaging disposition, charm and coquettishness are
more desirable in a wife than beauty and adornment.

Coquetry is not to vanquish the lover
A master should be mindful of his retainer.[9]

A houri of paradise with ugly manners is worse than a
demon; a maleficent demon with good manners would be
preferable.

A man with a wonderful house and wife
God's blessing is upon his life.[10]

Love requires charm and good manners as well as pleasing
ways and an engaging disposition.

Somebody criticized the Ghaznavid king,
I'm amazed his beloved Ayaz is not ravishing
He is like a flower that has neither color nor scent
On which a nightingale's love is totally misspent
Someone told the story to Mahmud, the king
He thought a while and said this is not a fling,
Sir, my love for him is for his character
Not for his pleasing form or stature.[11]

Ayaz was nothing but a slave. Therefore, a wife should try to
do her utmost to improve her manners and temperament to
please her husband.

In a wife look for manners and not beauty
Avoid a shrew even when she is like a houri

According to the Traditions, however, one should avoid both good and bad women, and one should absolutely not expect anything good or bad from them. You may expect something from a person who is intelligent, but God and the holy imams have said that women are deficient in intelligence. His Holiness the Commander of the Faithful, 'Ali son of Abu Talib (May the salvation of God be on him), made this disapproving pronouncement, "Be sure of this, O man, that woman is religiously, mentally, and legally an imperfect creature. As touching religion, she is forbidden to pray or fast during her monthly periods; as touching intelligence, the law demands the evidence of two women to that of one man; and as touching succession, the man receives the double of the woman. Carefully abstain, therefore, from bad women and flee from good ones. Never obey a woman, even when she counsels well, so that she lives in no hope of some day making you do evil."[12]

3. Old woman giving advice. From *Ta'dib al-Nesvan*.

4. Burden of Life. From *Ta'dib al-Nesvan*.

[The next paragraph provides a Persian translation of the previous one, which in the text is in Arabic. Then the text continues:]

Given these pronouncements of the Friend of God, what can you expect from women? Whatever this poor writer will add to this will but give rise to all kinds of curses and abuse that will be called upon this miscreant. But, as I have previously promised, I have written some chapters.

1

Of Women's Character and Conduct

This much is certain: that love should be mutual, and this cannot be compared with any other matter. A man who is in love with a woman, if he witnesses a lack of it, obviously he will forsake it if he has to complain without ceasing of its object; and when this happens, we may say with perfect truth that if the heart gains nothing by foregoing its affection, it loses nothing either. Suppose he encounters a thousand unkindnesses from his beloved because he has limited time [to see her], not more than one hour. For example, after some time, when during one hour the two lovers may see their love after a thousand obstacles, then he can behave in such a way that this one hour does not become a source of discord. You can behave in such a way for one hour or one day, but how can a person do so all this life? In companionship and association, all faults become evident and become the cause of a man's frustration. So the wife should behave in such a way not that there never will be any discourse between them, but rather that their love should increase hour by hour. Although longtime association and being together for a long period by itself creates lack of love, yet we have seen for many ugly and ill-shaped women, whose appearance displeases many, because of their good behavior and disposition their every fault appears to the husband as a thousand beauties, and never her defects are seen by the husband. Indeed,

The beloved is not the one with hair fine and waist
    shapely.
Be enamored of the beauty who has that special quality.[13]

Strangers and relatives express their surprise, saying, "It is
only because of his animal nature that he has a love for such
an ugly woman." That poor man, because he is well provided
for in every aspect, he suffers reproach and does not leave the
woman and says to her:

By your soul, if all the world comes to an end,
I cannot forget you for one moment.

Most of the time, it so happens, many beautiful, intelligent, and accomplished women are worse than poisonous
snakes and scorpions in the eyes of their husbands. That poor
man complains all the time about his bad luck. In order to
obtain his love, she does not know better than to go after the
potion of this molla or that Jewish sorcerer. What a wondrous
thing!

For many years, my heart sought the Holy Grail,
What was within myself, it sought from strangers to no
    avail.[14]

My lady, love is within yourself, and you are the reason for its
loss. The secret of why most ugly women succeed and often
are happy is partly because they despair of themselves, and
they compensate for their ugliness with good behavior and in
this way increase their husband's love.

I have plucked many fruits of desire from that palm of
    passion.
How can the tree of love give a fruit better than this?[15]

However, those poor beautiful souls who take pride in their natural beauty and are conceited about it and think that this is proper are overcome by the pride of beauty and forget good behavior. They are deceived by those who praise them and always say:

When hearing the beloved's pleasing words
The lover forgets heaven and earth.

The poor darlings are wrapped up in their conceit and vanity, and when they come to themselves, it is when their beauty is no longer the object of desire, and they are afflicted with pain and sorrow.

Fortune fled, heart burning and tearful eyes
My heart aflame, my eyes crying.

My dear, you should not be beguiled by beauty and comeliness; do not abandon good disposition. In any case and any circumstance be submissive and be self-effacing.

Until I have given up free will
I cannot join the dervish's whirl.[16]

The wife must completely efface herself when obeying her husband. She should not question anything and whatever he says she should do, for obeying her husband should be her duty.

I intend to recompense your cruelty with my soul.
I will continue to do so, else my life is not whole.[17]

If, for example, your husband causes you pain, bear it with open face. [A wife] should not for a moment shrink from executing her husband's orders because one moment of disobedience may constitute a year of discord.

> Either make no friends with elephant keepers
> Or build a house suitable for elephants.
> Either don't efface from your face the lover's blue
> Or put on a piety garb of mourners' hue.[18]

When the woman makes up her own mind and sees herself as the only one on the stage, and she considers herself the equal of her husband,[19] then she should not expect love from her husband unless she willingly and whole-heartedly obeys her husband and says, "My welfare is your welfare." This is a fine point, and among a hundred thousand women not one will be of such character. Of course, all this advice of mine is in vain—like catching moonlight, holding water in a sieve, or pounding air in a mortar. It is possible—nay, it is even certain—that when women gather around in their parties and see my remarks, they will say, "May he die young with this drivel that he has uttered, and may his beard be soaked with his blood. What nonsense So-and-So has written." They do not know that

> He who achieves his aim in this world
> Is one whose beloved with him is in accord.[20]

What a blessing it is when man and wife are of one heart and spend days and a few years of life in joy. Of necessity, the achievement of this task depends on women because it is they who will set all these affairs aright.

> O Hafez, your duty is to give advice.
> Don't be concerned whether it was heard or not.[21]

2

Control Your Tongue

Guarding your tongue is important because the wound of the tongue is worse than the wound of the spear.

> The soul-taking sword cannot do
> What the tongue can inflict on man.

The tongue has a strange impact, and it hurts worse than a sword's slash. Women should not utter bitter words at all; how well the poet has said:

> Bitter words from sweet lips are not becoming
> Speak sweetly that is the best of all things.[22]

Her words should be well-chosen and soothing;

> With sweet words you can always win,
> With bitter words you only cause clamor and din.[23]

Wounding words never heal, and as long as you live, they will leave a scar. Foolish the person who says a thousand wrong words, excusing himself that in a war you do not hand out sweet treats. Yes, my lady, it is a fight, and in a fight [your opponents] won't give sweet treats. In a fight, we use fists and feet, sticks and stones. But after the fight you cannot accept sweet treats from that wife, you cannot expect friendship. And you have to forget about your friendship. Whatever is said is imprinted on the table of your heart and like a festering sore is incurable.

Therefore, a wife should never utter a bitter word, and if she sees the husband in a bad temper, whether he be justified or not, she has to approach him as much as possible with kindness and softness to cool his temper. Good temper is like water on fire. Even if the fault was not hers, she should apologize and say, "I was wrong." If to this she subtly adds a few masterly caresses, her husband will become ashamed. If the husband will not be ashamed that moment, surely he will be so later on and in this way will love her more. It is better to say, "I did bad; I was wrong," than to stand up to the husband and raise up your hands and yell uncouth words at him and hear similar things from him that will ruin your relationship for years to come. The value of the wife is in the love for her husband, even if she is the daughter of a wealthy man and the man [who is her husband] a penniless stoker from the public baths. The more humility she shows, the better it is.

If by chance her husband's attitude does not change, she should excuse herself and go out until the atmosphere is changed. But she should not stay away long and should come back and try to make amends in whatever possible way. She should not utter a word that might create discord. To lift weights you need muscles. Great men have not been able to bear such a burden and have not been able to control their tongues. How then can women weak of heart and feeble in intelligence carry this load?

At any rate, a woman who seeks love and affection and who does not want to cut this amicable relationship has to suffer bitterness and be patient and has to stop wagging her sharp tongue. It is better than fighting and battling, which have no result but regret. As they say, patience is bitter, but will bear sweet fruits. In anger, you may lose your self-control and may utter bitter words that no needle can mend, and even if [husband and wife] make up, a trace of [this bitterness] will remain.

> There is no hope
> To repair a broken rope
> Without having a knot
> To mark its spot.[24]

The desired love is lost between them. The wife should not say, "My husband has said such and such thing, why should not I?" In not saying this, you will not be less of woman. Such thoughts are a sign of ignorance and a lack of decorum, and she will have distanced herself from her desired objective.

> Bid farewell to pleasure in a house
> Where the loud shouting is by the spouse.[25]
> Not traveling is better that having tight shoes,
> The hazards of travel better than at home having woes.[26]

With this, how can love and friendship remain? When the wife quarrels with her husband, then this is enmity, not friendship. Even if there were reconciliation, it would be like a truce between two enemies. As much as possible, she should not say unbecoming and uncouth words, even if they are in jest, because even in jest unbecoming words are not appropriate. She should never criticize her husband to his face, and she should not try to interrupt him; she should not complain either directly or indirectly. She should absolutely avoid sending messages because one word leads to another. She should never complain about her husband in conversation with strangers. It has happened many times that the same words in a different context will be said by that person supposedly in a friendly manner, but they will actually be worse than when said by an enemy.

3

Do Not Complain

A wife should never complain about her husband, even if she has a hundred reasons to do so. Complaints will give rise to complaints. The root cause of complaints is coldness, and, however close the relationship may be, complaints end in grief. What have wife and husband to complain about?

As His Majesty, the King of Kings,[27] has written:

> It is not pleasant to see your beautiful face whining.
> Seeing your face is a pleasure when it is not complaining.[28]

Truly, as the saying goes, "The word of the king is the king of words."

This poem indicates that complaining is absolutely unbecoming; if there has to be any complaining, it should be by old women about young brides. If husband and wife do not care much for each other, it does not matter, but if they love one another, then complaining is out of place and unbecoming. Complaints gradually result in fights, and there is no resolution in sight. I have seen many ladies who are particularly fond of making gratuitous complaints and are always looking for pretexts to lash out.

> A wife told a khan, "although I've no reason to complain
> But what to do when I don't have the patience to abstain?"
>
> You said, "You do not want to get laid."
> No, no, that's wrong. You don't have an active blade.

Now, if they complain kindly and softly, then there is no problem. But God forbid if they raise their voice and bray like she-asses and then say, "This is the way we talk." Shouting in a loud voice is not at all becoming, and as the Koran says, "The worst of sounds is the sound of the donkey."[29] Do not think that having a loud voice is a good thing, and do not listen to those flatterers who say, "Bravo, your voice sounds like a fire-spouting cannon"; it is better to realize that these compliments are ridiculous.

Therefore, the wife should never complain, should never interrupt or utter ugly and uncouth words, and should not even think of contradicting her husband. And when she is talking, she should not imagine herself championing a cause, should not waive her hands about and put them in all directions, so the poor husband sitting close by may not be injured by the lady's fists. She should not with eyes protruding out of their sockets and her mouth foaming, her arms jerking around like a boxer's, rocking from one leg to another, raise dust to the seventh heaven and pour forth poisonous words.

Rather, the beauty and grace of a woman show when she talks softly and quietly, her voice being as weak and delicate as if she has risen from the sickbed. With incredible coquettishness and indescribable elegance, she moves her finger; she does not look this or that way, but with downcast eyes, with gentleness and grace she utters infatuating and loving words; sometimes she touches her skirt. In her speech and in her behavior, she should act in such a way that her gentility and coquettishness draws the attention of every eye and ear. If she is quiet for a while, everyone desires her to speak again, and the husband with heart and soul is eager for her words. If he has a thousand laments and sorrows, they would be effaced with her tender

words, and the rust of trouble would be rubbed away from his
heart. He would say with a thousand supplications:

> There is no stranger among us; speak out,
> Except the taper whose tongue I will soon cut.[30]

Woe to me, woe to me, what am I saying? None of these
words will please the ladies, but I am writing them to do my
duty, although these statements are not for writing and discussion. Rather, the wife should be a conscientious researcher
and observe all these things and educate herself to acquire
the manners that I have explained. She should not tell herself,
"This is my character; I am ill-tempered, ill-tongued, my voice
is harsh, I cannot restrain myself, and God has created me in
this way. Go and get a wife that is better than I; this is the way
I am." My answer is:

> Take my advice or your own way;
> I have said all I had to say.[31]

All these ideas come from foolishness and lack of intelligence, for most human behavior is acquired and not innate.
If ignorance is not perpetuated, she will understand her fault
and will become aware of its ugliness and will abandon it. Bitterness is changed to sweetness, copper to gold, and therefore
I preach the alchemy of proper behavior. Whoever wants can
turn her essence into pure gold. If not, it is her choice; she
knows best.

4

No Sulking

A wife should never sulk, however much hardship she has to endure; she has to see the positive side and be patient. I have heard it said that an old woman, when she was on the verge of death, may God bless her, expressed as her last wish to her daughter—and what good advice it was—"My child, promise me never to sulk with your husband in regard to these two things: the table and the bed. For if you refuse to eat, you sulk against your belly, and that is annoying; and if you refuse a cover, you will catch a cold, which is harmful."

Apart from the old woman's last wish, sulking gradually engenders hatred and enmity. Therefore, a wife should never sulk, frown, or look sullen.

> Better be in the judge's prison in disgrace
> Than sit at home looking at a sullen face.[32]

The wife should be cheerful, happy, and joyous, and she should talk nicely and smile. She should not sulk and grieve all the time like old mourning widows who sit with their hands under their chins or with their arms folded, with a face more sour than vinegar and more pungent than garlic, as if their steamboat[33] had gone down, or as if they had labored from morn till dusk to win bread for their husbands.

My dear lady, what is the problem? What has happened? By God, even if in beauty you were equal to the light of the moon or in virtue second to none, someone who is on his deathbed would not take the water of life from your hands if you were in such a mood. In such a situation, what do you expect? What pleasure can you enjoy?

The poor husbands, each according to his standing, who have done lawful and unlawful things and have suffered many humiliations for your sake from morn till evening, when they come to their wretched home, they hope to have a moment of peace so that they may find relief from the daily cares. Woe to the poor husband if, as is the custom of shrewish wives, as soon as he sets his foot in the house, he is greeted with recriminations, shouts, and grimaces.

> From a vixen wife protect us well,
> Save us, O God, the pains of hell.[34]

5

Of Bearing and Behavior in Society

A wife should not walk fast, should hold her head high and not bend her back, and her gait should be graceful. She should walk slowly in such a way that her entire movement is nice and elegant.

> Wherever you go, a flame of our love shines
> Wherever you look, your moonlike beauty shows.[35]

Not like the streetwalkers who turn their head and hips when they walk. A wife should pay great attention to the way she walks and moves. She should walk and behave gracefully, attractively, alluringly, lovingly, and nicely so that all will say, "Who is that lady? When she goes away, it is as if our soul departs."

In walking, she should not move her hands excessively; at the same time, she should keep them glued to her side like sticks; it is not necessary to move her bottom like a grinding millstone because when she is walking, it will move naturally; tasteless and exaggerated movements of the hips are the manner of public women who are looking for a customer. It has nothing to do with the world of coquetry; only gracefulness is needed in walking. A woman should walk in such a way that would be suitable to this poem:

When seated, she's the bright moon rising
When rising, she's a cypress straight standing
Like a willow, she takes pride in her stately shape
She has risen to kill me, whose heart is agape.

In this manner, when she enters and sits down at a party, everybody will praise and admire her. She should not spit or pick her nose, which is very bad and disgusts people. She should be aware that there should not be any sleep in the corner of her eyes or nothing dried up coming out of her nose. She should take a little, soft handkerchief and occasionally clean her eyes and nose so that she will not offend others without knowing it, like old women and widows in whose eyes there is tons of sleep and from whose mouths and noses saliva is dripping, which looks absolutely disgusting. When sneezing or coughing, she should cover her nose and mouth with the handkerchief so that the spittle is not spread, especially if a poor soul is sitting next to her; he should not be drenched. He has not done anything to deserve being sprayed with spit and drivel instead of rose water, as he should.

It is clear what he will say to himself and what kind of resentment will be the result of it. In particular, when she is talking, she should be very considerate, and when she comes and sits by her husband, she should not throw herself down in such a way that the dust raises to heaven, but rather sit down so gracefully that the husband will say:

O my soul, you are impressive from top to toe; I confess
What a craftsman is God, having made such perfection out
    of nothingness
Nowhere have I seen the sun in a moving cypress
Neither tongue nor pen can do justice to your loveliness.[36]

When she sits at her husband's side, she should not take up all the room, but rather kneel at a little distance from him. Then, if this position eventually tires her, she has only to rise up, walk about a little and come back or go somewhere else and lie down for a moment so that her fatigue will go away. What she must not do is wrap herself in her chador and begin snoring, nor must she squat down and cuddle her knees with her arms as if she were a widow and inconsolable. She should sit properly as if she were happy and occasionally fondly press her husband's hand so that the husband may occasionally put his arm around her waist.

> Sometimes he kisses her ravishing eyes
> Sometimes she gives him her disheveled tresses.[37]

She should talk gently and softly and entertain her husband so that even if they are together from eve to morn, there won't be any boredom, but rather she will make him desire her more. She should not interrupt her husband, and while he is speaking, she should pay attention to what he says. And it is better to sit next to the husband rather than face him.

> There is no pleasure being face to face
> My beloved should be next to me, that's her place.

When she wants to get up, she should do so gently and not like pregnant women, who put their hands down and lift themselves up.

> When she sits down, the turmoil of the city does the same.
> When she rises up, a thousand fires of desire are aflame.

It is better not to sit next to the stove so that her face is roasted or smothered in smoke. It is better to have the room heated rather than sit under the *korsi*[38] because doing so makes the complexion yellow and makes her look sickly. She should not sit in the sun, as do old women, who whenever they find a sunlit spot sit there mournfully and wrapped in thought as if they have lost many of their dear ones.

She must not be without eye shadow and must use rouge, but not excessively, so her face will look natural, not like the red bottom of monkeys; she should not color her lips and cheeks and even her eyes and nose thinking that she has to make herself like a bouquet of flowers. In Europe, they make little use of rouge, powder, and makeup. Surely, what God has created is better than artificial embellishment.

Of course, the ladies will say, "If you are right, why do they manufacture so much makeup in Europe and export it to Iran?" To which I reply, "First, it is made for wrinkled old women in Iran and to get money. Second, it is for the old women of Europe." If a woman is young and is blessed with beauty, there is no need for rouge or powder. God forbid, if the age of the lady rises a bit and she loses her natural beauty, whatever she does will be in vain anyway.

> It is of no use to adorn the eyebrow for the blind.
> A lovely maid needs no makeup artist, she's one of a kind.[39]

Yes, rouge is fine for those ladies whose color is naturally pale, but in such small amounts that the color looks like the natural color of the skin. But what is the use of a red nose? What good does it do? You should apply only a little rouge so that nobody will see the difference between the natural color and that of the rouge. If God has given a woman black eyebrows, there is no need to apply antimony, and if she does not have enough eyebrows, only then she should apply it. But it should not be very thick.

Do not let stray hair grow on the face and say that "So-and-So, a friend of mine, lets it grow." There is no need to pluck it out every two weeks; once every two months is enough. In short, it is better not to let your face hair grow.

> O let the heart, by fatal absence rent,
> Feel what I think, and bleed when I lament
> My secrets are not alien from my plaintive notes,
> Yet the sensual eye and ear do not take note.[40]

6

How to Eat

A wife should sit at the tablecloth on her two knees, while smiling and not chattering. She should partake of each dish, whether bad or good, with a smiling face and in small morsels. She should eat with her fingertips, in particular with her thumb and two fingers. She should not put large pieces into her mouth and should not chew too quickly so that half of the food comes out of her mouth or so that her mouth is so full she cannot breathe but through her nose.

She must eat small bites in such a way that the sound of her chewing is not heard a mile away. She should take each piece daintily and avoid bad-smelling or flatulent dishes so that her belching, either from above or below, occur not together; it does not make any difference whether it is the smell of radish or cabbage or wind from the belly. She should put aside ill temper and dispute because if the food is not good, it cannot be replaced at that moment. She can express her displeasure after the meal is finished. I have heard and seen some women who save up their anger and express it at the table.

If the husband complains of bad cooking, the wife should calm him down with pleasant words so that they can eat at least a few morsels in peace. She should not begin to knock the bowls against the jars and the jars against the bowls. A woman sometimes breaks the plates or throws the bread or tears up the tablecloth, screaming, "Bring the servant, call the housekeeper, take away the tutor, and bring in the *farrash*[41] with his sticks!" She sometimes slaps the children on the head, saying, "Eat properly!" If, for example, a poor innocent four-year-old asks for something, she shouts and curses him: "Pox on you!" or "Clap on you!" "What a little glutton you are, may you die." And she makes so much fuss and swears so much that the poor child comes to tears and leaves the table without eating. In this situation, the food is stuck in the mouth of the poor husband, and to resolve the situation he recites the *Ayat al-korsi*[42] and wishes a thousand times that he would die of hunger and not be at such a table or vows that he would rather eat barley bread than touch such food.

> Leave the table when you're not welcome,
> For staying means a loss of honor and is loathsome.[43]

Oh good Lord, why cannot a woman sit down nicely with her husband and eat the food in peace and quiet, as if it is a dish from heaven, and then smilingly and pleasantly get up?

> Thanking God for his bounty may increase your share
> Ingratitude for what you receive will take away your fare.[44]

Nothing is worse than a woman's ill temper at the table, although it is unbecoming from anybody. But because I am writing this piece about women, this point is particularly addressed to them. Food eaten in this way is fouler than a dog's blood. It is unfortunate that people around the table have to suffer; the lady of the house is furious, the cook is trembling, and the husband wants to get away. Such food, how can it be enjoyed? Of course, it won't be. Poison would be better than such food.

It has been observed that some ladies, on account of their innate nobility, under these circumstances don't eat anything except bread and cheese or some snacks for a few days. Well, my lady, would not it be better if you neither displayed such a temper nor made other people's life miserable nor starved yourself?

O my heart, if you covet the light of your soul,
For a moment close your mouth and exercise self-control.

7

Of Bodily Cleanliness and the Use of Certain Perfumes

Nothing is more unattractive in a woman than to make use of animal fat for her head, face, and hands. There is no point in smelling like a greasy cook. She should not touch grease, even when it is a cosmetic and made with one thousand kilos of rose water, for if it contains fat, it will be filthy. When somebody uses fat, she does not realize what kind of smell she gives off. Grease, wax, and oil were good enough for the late princes Vali and Shah Qoli Khan, who knew how to use it properly, but it is not good for one who wants to be the beloved of the husband. The wife should not listen to the stupid counsel of this or that lady and should not use any fat for her hair. It is most certain that fat does not increase the thickness of hair, but it makes it grow long. In all honesty, long hair, especially for those who have fine hair, is not good at all; fine hair looks like a pony's tail. If it is hair that is thick, it is good; otherwise, long fine hair that is braided or thrown around the shoulders is not beautiful. It is better that she should cut her hair short if it is not very thick, and it will be much better that her hair falls around her face, and each strand of it will capture the heart.

> Don't leave your tresses so uncurled
> Your beauty will create turbulence in the world.[45]

However, using perfume is very good. A woman should always scent her dresses; she should always use good-smelling powders and good scents to increase love and passion; it is better than any ornament. But [she should] not [do] like the Arabs, who put musk among their clothes, because musk gives one a headache.

Using perfume and rose water is very good, provided that it does not create an allergy in the husband or provided he does not have a cold. In such a case, she should not use it at all.

Dyeing your hair with henna is good. The smell of henna is sometimes pleasurable, but putting it on your hand is bad; especially after one day passes, its color becomes dirty. That is, some men enjoy it when the fingernails or tips are dyed with henna, whereas some don't like it. Tastes are different. But in my view, nothing is better than natural colors for hands and feet. If the color red was good for them, God would have made them so. God has created a freshness in the color of the body of a woman and of her arms and legs, which in itself is beyond description.

> When that ravishing idol bares her legs and arms,
> I feel the muse of passion working her charms.[46]

Since God has created the color of your hands so beautifully, you should attend to them so that they stay clean, and definitely every day at least you should wash them with soap and water. The soap should be perfumed, not the bad smelling kind.

She should not dirty her hands, and she should not touch the things that blacken the hands, even if it may be dust. She should keep her hands so tender that they are a nice place to imprint a kiss. They should not be in such a state that nobody will have the desire to look at them. She should at least put on silk gloves, even when she is sitting under the *korsi*. If her hands become dirty and untidy, it is obvious that the husband will not be inclined to touch her. But if they are beautiful and clean, then everybody will love to hold them and even eat them.

If the Saki pours the wine with that tender hand,
It will make all the saints eternal drunkards in the land.[47]

8

Concerning How to Dress

A woman should always wear clean clothes, and she should not show herself to her husband in dirty, greasy, and old clothes. She should dress like a peacock showing off. She should change her attire once a day, especially her shirt—maybe even twice per day, but if that is not possible, once. She should not become accustomed to her own odor because one does not smell it on oneself. In winter, she should change at least every two days, and in summer twice a day, but if that's not possible, once a day.

She should not imitate others because "such and such ladies have done this or that, and I should do likewise." It is true; imitation is allowed. She may imitate others provided the husband likes it. Otherwise, she should leave it and should not insist, "How come such and such lady is doing it, and why should not I?" To argue that because some other woman dresses up or wants to throw herself off the roof, you may do the same is utterly absurd. She may be in the wrong, though she is not blamed for it, and you put yourself in the wrong by following her.

The objective of good or bad is to please the husband and gain his affection. If something does not please the husband, even if it is good, it should not be done. I have seen ladies, present company excluded, who forced their poor husbands to buy all sorts of dresses and accessories, and they never wear them. The dresses and the jewelry stay in the closet or are worn only when they go to parties. One should be fair: the wretched husband has bought them at great expense and effort, so at least wear it for his sake twice a year. It is his dear desire that you should have the best in the world, not only of clothes, but also of wit and beauty. Don't you see that whatever husbands see, they express the desire, "I wish my wife to have it," or "I wish my wife to have this quality."

However, God has not created everyone with the same tastes. For example, one husband likes short dresses, but another prefers long ones. The wife of this one should wear a short dress, and the other one should put on the dress that pleases her husband. She should try to please her husband's taste.

There are many husbands who per force have said, "Yes, yes," and approved of their wives' behavior and even praised them excessively, or, according to the custom, in order to protect their wives from the evil eye, they have burned wild rue or a small piece of the cord of their underpants in the fire.[48] And they recite this poem by Sa'di, who says:

> Against the evil eye either cover your face
> Or burn wild rue in a fire ablaze.[49]

The wife does not really understand that all of this is but a show put up to keep the peace. Therefore, she smiles secretly, saying to herself: "All this is because I am so good, pretty, and beautiful." However, when she has left, the husband thanks God many times and says, "I've fooled her! I got rid of her," and utters a thousand reprehensible words regarding her qualities and faults. So what use are false words? Words should be heartfelt and feel good, and he should not be forced to lie.

If a husband says, "I am not afraid of women," he is either lying or lacking in intelligence because, first of all, man has to be afraid of a creature who is defect in reason. Second, how can he not be apprehensive of his wife when his honor, his property, his life, his children, and even his soul are in her hands? We cannot change our wives every moment as we change a shirt or underwear. Therefore, a wife is the companion for life. One should pray to God that her disposition and behavior are good; otherwise, we will be afflicted for life, and we will have to suffer and endure.

> O Qa'ani, close your lips from vain conversation.
> This dispute is but pure fantasy and waste of imagination.[50]

O God, remove all evil from the affairs of Moslems.

Going back to our own discussion: When a well-bred wife hears her husband's dislike regarding her dress or another matter, she immediately tries to correct this. And she should be pleased that he expressed it instead of sulking and sitting with a sour face. If, for example, the husband says, "Your petticoats are a little bit short," she should not become annoyed and break pots and pans, sulk, or answer by yelling a thousand reproaches, saying: "What do you want of me? Leave me alone. Go and get another wife. This is who I am. I am bad, May God kill me, God has made me so. You cannot change me."

After she has made many idiotic remarks, the poor husband has to eat his own words. And he thinks, "What a blunder I've made. I tried to make it better, and it became worse. I wanted to do something about the length of my wife's petticoat, and I ruined all my chances."

He starts to apologize profusely. He is mindful of the anger of the lady and says, "I am sorry, I made a mistake; I did not mean your petticoat. You misunderstood." And after that he is forced to lie all the time and continue to praise her and continue dissimulating. Of course, the lady's heat has not subsided. He is forced, without having an inclination to do so, to make love to her so that the lady's heat may abate. If, God forbid, intercourse does not take place, then he has to flee. Both sides have to suffer all these adversities but for a sensible word that is never heeded.

> When two sides are friends, things are well
> Like two almonds in one shell.

Now, if there is no further foolishness and there is friendship, she should understand that if her husband is saying that he is finding fault with his wife, it is out of friendship, not out of enmity.

> Only a true friend tells your defects
> Like a shining mirror as it reflects.[51]

If the woman is intelligent and understanding and desires to fulfill the husband's wishes, there won't be any disagreement and unhappiness between them ever. Even if they live together hungry and thirsty for many years, being content with barley bread and a pitcher of water, with their mutual love they will spend their life in happiness and joy.

> It's not great fun being at the world's party.
> I have tried its wine—it is not very hearty.

Let us not allow our brief lives to be spent in conflict and bitterness. One desires the other's death in secret, and the other tries to free himself. Such friendship is worse than a thousand enmities.

All this comes from stupidity and incompatibility. All this comes from the wife's ill temper. The wife should attract the husband like a magnet so that he cannot rest without her for a moment.

Nearly every domestic misfortune is owing to lack of intelligence on the wife's part. But however foolish she may be, she can at least use love as a loadstone to draw her husband's heart and to attach it utterly.

> With half a glance, a hundred realms of heart you can buy.
> In this deal the fair ones are awry.[52]

Of course, it is true.

> If the beloved does not give the lover a thought,
> The trials of the poor lover are all for naught.

Love is coincidental and acquired. It comes forth from a little affection and disappears with the slightest dispute. The belief that maintains that love remains until death and that we are steady in love is but a lie. Just ask me, the old, experienced man. By God, in spite of expressing that unimaginable love for the husband on the day he dies, the wife starts looking for a suitable [new] husband among the pallbearers who have come to take the corpse. Although she is pretending to mourn, she wants to find out who would be a strong and proper husband for her. This may be true for good women, but as to the rest I seek refuge in God.

It is related that God gave Solomon and his wife, Bilqis [the queen of Sheba], a handicapped child. Solomon was saddened. The angel Gabriel came down and said, "If you, your minister, Asaf ben Barkhiya, and your wife express whatever is in your hearts, God will cure this child." Then all three turned in the direction of Mecca. First, Solomon said, "O God, you bear witness that with all this kingdom that I have, if two complainants come to me with a dispute and one of them brings me an apple, even if he is not right, I am tempted to favor his case, although he may be in the wrong, so that he may depart in joy and be content with me."

Then the vizier Asaf said, "O God, in spite of the fact that I have so much power, sometimes I think of what would happen if I were the king and not be subject to Solomon's authority."

Bilqis said, "O God, you know that although I am the wife of the King of the World, the Ruler over men and jinnis, I sometimes, when I see a young man more handsome than he, I wish that he would be as handsome and young as him." God cured the child. Although I have not seen this story in a book and have only heard it from people, if this story be true and Bilqis, who was allegedly endowed with such virtue and honor, behaved in this way, what can you expect from other women?

Yes, as long as there is love, as they say, faults appear as virtues in the eyes of the lover. Good qualities have a life of their own. So the wife should behave in such a way that love does not become affected and [instead] covers all faults. Everlasting love is a veil over all imperfections. Once love is gone, it will never return.

> Don't hurt this wild bird of my heart
> Lest it fly away and forever depart.[53]

In short, the wife should try to be sincere and pure of heart and neither be proud of her beauty nor listen to flatterers so that she may not regret the outcome and will have to say, "I did wrong and wasted my life."

> Before time bends your stature into a bow,
> O cypresslike youth, play in the world's meadow.[54]

9

Of Bed and Sleeping Manners

This is the whole point that I have been trying to make, and this chapter is the most important one. When night falls and it is time to sleep, this most important chapter opens. All the preparations, the hustle and bustle, are for resting at night. God has created night for repose and comfort. If the night were like the day, how miserable that would be.

> The day is for achievements, and drinking in daytime
> Will cause your mirror-like heart to rust in dark grime.
> The time for drinking morning—like wine—is the night
> When night pitches its tent, horizon's pavilion is out of
>   sight.[55]

At night, one should be busy with one's own world and find enjoyment and comfort in it. The gathering of friends happens at night, and one takes the joy of life with one's beloved at night.

The best of joys in the world is sleeping. Have you ever imagined how if a person is awake at night but sleeps from morning till evening, he cannot enjoy one hour's pleasure of nightly rest? Resting at night is good, but it has conditions.

Women have made a great mistake in supposing that the source of love is sleeping together in bed. Surely the origin of this notion is those hateful old women who, like dragons and leviathans, devour men and who first conceived this miserable idea of a bed for two. And now the force of routine has made the use of such things general. It has remained as a custom.

If a woman sleeps apart from her husband, in the morning all of these aunties and flatterers and so-called vegetable cleaners (hangers-on) sit around her mournfully and heave deep sighs of grief, saying: "Our dear daughter has become unlucky and unfortunate. She sleeps alone at night. Was it only for a mouthful of bread that she came to this house? She could have had the same in her parents' house."[56]

With such talk, they ruin the life of the poor husband and destroy the realm of love so that he never dares to sleep alone at night again and so that this kind of talk will not be repeated.

> A night of waiting is not a year, my dear.
> After all, it is only a night, not a year.

It is a great mistake for the couple in love, like Leyla and Majnun, to sleep together all the time, for, according to the saying of wise men and physicians and those experienced in the affairs of love, this will decrease affection and engender hatred.

It has been recorded in books by philosophers that a doctor was asked, "Someone is exceedingly in love and has abandoned everything and is always busy with the beloved. Whatever we do, his love increases hour by hour." The doctor said, "Arrange for them to share one bed and let their breath mingle, for then their passion will decrease, and the heat of love will turn into dislike." They did exactly what the doctor ordered, and the love of the lovers abated. Especially when people inhale each other's breath, it causes aversion.

Furthermore, God has not created all human beings the same way so that they sleep at the same time and get up at the same time or are exactly of the same humor, in cold or heat, in sickness and health. You see one sleeping while the other one is awake. The one who is awake grumbles; the other one becomes cold, and the other feels warm. One cannot breathe properly, and the other one snores; one gets up early, the other one late; one sneezes, and the other one does not. Because of all these different reactions, sharing one bed engenders aversion and dislike.

If the wife is one of these old and ugly women who is not worthy of being a beloved and forces herself upon her husband with petulance and all sorts of unbecoming means and wants the husband to be henpecked and an absolute slave to her, he is forced to share the same bed whether he wants to or not.

> Though I'm feeble and weak as an ant,
> I still breathe and under your burden I pant.[57]

If the husband dares to turn away from the wife, he will be punched on the head and in the ribs and kicked not only out of the bed, but also out of the house. The poor man, what can he do in the middle of the night, especially in winter? Where can he go? He has no choice but to return and kiss the wife's feet and embrace her until morning, even though doing so may be torture in itself. He has to fulfill the lady's desire; otherwise, there is no way out.

Present company excluded, I have seen some stupid and foolish wives who insist on sharing the same bed with their husbands. They absolutely insist on sleeping in the same bed with their husband, and if the poor man expresses some displeasure, they angrily say, "If a wretched, smelly harlot were here, you would embrace her all night; when it comes to me, you do not like it. You men are really bastards; you like loose women." They don't realize that this wretched, smelly harlot, who, according to them, might be a concubine, leaves if you tell her to leave, and she does whatever you tell her to do. If you say "sleep," she sleeps. If you say "go," she goes. That is why a man sometimes likes them; otherwise, how is it possible for a husband to appreciate the love of his own wife, who is his noble paternal cousin or his noble maternal cousin?

If the lady wants the husband to embrace her willy-nilly and say flattering words, the wretched husband has to obey. But if she really desires true love and friendship and wants to remain beloved, she should forget about these stories and not listen to anyone's advice. She should not always share the bed with her husband, even when the husband insists and persists. When the wife is well behaved and is liked by her husband, she should not give in even though the husband insists. However, sharing one's bed gradually decreases love, and therefore she should not accept at all to do so. Obviously, her refusal will increase his love for her. Man is desirous of what has been forbidden to him. When man and wife are asleep, what difference does it make whether they are in one bed or not? While they are awake, being together is desirable, so that they love each other even more. But while they are asleep, they obviously are not aware of each other.

That is why I am suggesting that a good wife should have her bed separate from that of her husband, and she should change her clothes and should wear nothing but a soft and a delicate chemise; she should not put on a vest. If she has to wear one, it should be a soft and light one. She should not fill her pockets with stuff and make them like the bag of Molla Qotb, the magician, who can make anything appear from his pocket that he needs from it. She should not put on a headscarf and tighten it under her chin with a pin, a needle, or something like that, but wear nothing more than a skullcap. As I said, people have different tastes. If the husband likes it, she should wear a thin, gauzy headscarf. If she has short hair, so much the better. But if she has long hair and tresses, she should be mindful that they are not under her body and wrapped around her arms and neck. She should perfume, clean, and beautify herself when she wants to get into her bed.

> If such a nimble beauty were to come within my fold,
> I would tell her how she needed to be consoled.

In bed, she should not roll from one side to the other like a heavy rock, but rather move gracefully like a light bird. If the husband wants to enter her bed or call her to his bed, she should go there with pleasure. She should not overdo coquetry and should not say unpleasant words, but rather she should join him with grace and warmth in his bed or receive him in her bed and be playful and converse pleasantly. She should not show reserve because "my husband has not yet touched me," for now is not the time for such thoughts.

In bed, one should never mention daily happenings and complaints or bring up unpleasant subjects or senseless requests. A wife should say nice, passionate words and should not refrain from kissing and foreplay. Sometimes she should be on her side, sometimes under him, sometimes on the other side, but all the time kisses and playfulness should be indulged in. All is foreplay, action and reaction. There is no room for prudishness and shame in bed. She should go forth with absolute audacity and should forget about the notion that "I am a lady and should not behave in this manner." So, my lady, what of your station? If you do not like it, why did you marry?

Between the sheets, a couple cannot always be like Leyla and Majnun, but at the same time the husband should not treat her like the courtesan Bibi Khatun Jan Qohpayeh either.[58] In short, in bed she should not hold back anything and should act with grace, passion, agility, and nice moves.

> I rise up laughing and fall on you anon
> While my Mars eclipses your Moon
> I inhale your fragrance and perfume myself on and on
> Time and again, I kiss you and eat sugar from your lips
>   aswoon.

Daily reality should absolutely not be brought into nightly affairs and words. The couple should behave as if they have not seen each other except that night.

During the day, she should not sit, as is the custom of the women of our time, and tell everything of what happened last night and sometimes show all her friends the marks she may have had on the neck or breast, saying: "Look how fortunate I am." Curse be on you and such a good fortune. What good fortune? Fortunate is she who does not behave in such a manner.

There are some bad-mannered and vulgar women who write to their friends in another part of the city, "Last night my husband said such and such and did such and such." Or they get together in the public baths, talk with friends and strangers alike, eat some pickled eggplants and bread, and say, "Last night my husband did it ten times with me," and they think that they have come to the public bath of glorification. God's and the Prophet's curses be on such women. The talk of bed should remain in bed. She should not even tell the husband what he did or said because he already knows what he has done and said. They should embrace each other like sweet souls, and if it lasts till morning, what a blessing.

> Tonight when my sweet beloved holds me tight
> If like aloe she sets fire to me, it won't be a plight.[59]

From the beginning of getting together, one should not talk of lovemaking so that foreplay thereafter, as is commonly said, is like a kiss after ejaculation. Even if the husband should insist, it is better that the wife should show a little bit of reluctance on every occasion because copulation ruins foreplay and pleasure, but not to such an extent that the poor man goes flaccid. Reluctance should be combined with coquetry and tenderness, not with donkeylike movements and kicking. In play and talk, she should be soft and gracious. The lamp should be extinguished, and, of course, chaperons and storytellers should not be present; in such a world, even underwear is a stranger.

> Between us there won't be but a single shift.
> If that is a barrier, I will tear it away and be swift.[60]

As soon as they are tired of playing and sleeplessness, the wife should go to her own bed and leave the husband to rest. If, after having slept, he gets up and desires the wife, she should not coquettishly say, "Am I your slave girl or concubine who comes at your command to play with you?" At this time, she is a respected permanent wife, not a friend, spiritual or otherwise. Some men are infatuated with vulgar concubines. This is why the wife should not act so haughtily. She should be ready whenever the husband wants her and in whatever manner, even if she is in the restroom or the vestibule of the house. Whenever husbands ask for such women, these women are always ready, wherever it happens to be. And they would not say in the way of an apology, "Cannot we do it in a better place?" Our friend Hajji Jahandar Mirza used to call the concubines "Madam Ever Ready."

The essential thing in this context is lovemaking, and all these preparations and fuss are for its sake. Don't you see that all these preliminaries, show, and ado are for lovemaking?

At a wedding, they take the bride with music and drums and a group of men and women to the house of the bridegroom, and then they sit outside waiting for the heroic bridegroom to perform his act. If he tarries a while, everybody laughs, and if they could, they would turn the groom's dress into a funereal one. And if the act does not happen between the husband and wife for two days, and even if he displays a thousand signs of affection and love, it is all in vain, but after the act, if the man breaks the woman's head, she says, "It was in jest," and she endures and shows patience. Before the copulation, if the husband is nice and endearing because he has not done it, the wife may become angry and say: "You are laughing at me." Such behavior is not counted as a shortcoming for women.

Upon this act depends the reproduction of the human species. If God did not make us subject to lust, how would the woman, after enduring pregnancy for nine months and giving birth and suffering in doing so, be inclined to this act again, or how would a husband, after knowing that a child has come out from that place, ever again be willing to have intercourse with her? Therefore, this act is God's providence for reproduction of the human species. If one looks at it objectively, it is a disgusting act, for one enters one pissing instrument into another one. But how much sufferance and how much pleasure one gets from it. Therefore, man has no choice but to do it. Although this act decreases love, if it does not happen, one should take refuge in God.

There is a famous Turkish proverb purporting that the wife says, "Don't give me bread, don't give me water, don't give me clothes, but don't lack in love."

The relationship between husband and wife can be of two kinds. In the first kind, the husband is a captive in the hands of a shrewish, ill-tempered, and lustful wife. He has no choice but to be henpecked, beaten up, and he has to be at the lady's beck and call in order to avoid being cursed, beaten, or divorced. He has to act according to his wife's desires, not his own. In the second kind, the wife and husband are extremely affectionate and have sex out of mutual desire.

A good wife should not be after preliminaries. It has been observed that when they become respectable permanent wives and when the poor man wants to have sex during daytime, then a special place has to be prepared. The servant has to come, spread the bed, lay the towel, and close the door. Then the lady has to get undressed, but by this time the poor man may have no desire anymore and has perhaps fallen asleep already. And if he does not fall asleep and does not go flaccid, neither husband nor wife know what they are doing. So the wife should not want such things, and whenever the husband, day or night, has an inclination to play and have intercourse, she should be ready, and she should not say "no" because she will regret it.

At that moment, she should not be lacking in coquetry and tender behavior, lustful gestures, and she should not be at all ashamed so that they both will not regret later having missed these things. The more provocative and tender she behaves, the more desirous, loved, and endeared she will be.

After the accomplishment of intercourse, she should go pleased to her own bed and rest. When they get up in the morning, as I explain in the forthcoming chapter, the lady should get up before the husband and should not occupy herself with the husband. She should leave him to the servants so that he can wash up and come to breakfast.

> O Sa'di, you waste your life by too much talk.
> It is time to apologize and say: God forgive us all.[61]

10

Of Waking and Rising Manners

When the wife gets up in the morning, after saying her prayers, she should not prolong reading the Koran and saying prayers, but without delay she should comb her hair, apply eye shadow, sprinkle her hair and face with rose water, and come to the husband with a smiling face like a flaunting pheasant and a shining moon. In the morning, she should not get up and with sleepy eyes, smudged eye shadow and dirty color rouge, unbrushed teeth, smelly breath, and dirty crumpled clothes sit next to the husband in an unswept room, continuously yawning. For then the poor husband's day is already benighted with her appearance, her sleepiness, the smell of garlic and burned tobacco of the water pipe, and he wishes a thousand times for a refuge from this hellish existence, and he leaves, trying to find succor outside of the house.

The lady imagines that she should not be separate from the husband for a moment and is expecting that he should kiss and smell her. Truly, your lady, you are right. The husband at that time should lick the sleep from your eyes like sugar candy and like a dog lick your face. If he goes away, even for a minute, what mistake has he made? Such a mistake that neither Molla Ghaffar, the preacher, nor Sheikh Musa, the sorcerer,[62] could set aright in a hundred years.

As I have said, it is necessary for the wife that she should get up before the husband, and before showing her face to the husband, she should go to the other room, do her makeup, and beautify herself; and even if the husband gets up before her, she should cover her face and go out of the room. She should not imagine that "it is no big deal that he should see me in this state" and should not assume that if someone loves his wife, he should not care for these details. Imagining this is an absolute mistake; love does not come from our mother's womb. The outside appearance counts greatly, and one should do anything that creates this pleasure. One should not displease the husband.

She should at least brush her teeth in the morning and should not say, "My crystal teeth are clean as pearls, and my breath is better than the smell of a rose." This may be the case, but it may be that at night the bile of the humor has increased, and the poor husband, when he wants to kiss your blessed mouth, becomes so disgusted with your bad breath that even if he were a thousand times in love with you, that love will go away. She should not think that even though such and such a man's wife has bad breath, her husband nevertheless kisses her day and night all the time and sucks her tongue. The purpose of what I am writing and saying is to teach, not to investigate or to argue.

When you go to the restroom, you have no choice but to put up with bad smell, and there is no escape from it. But sitting with your wife should not be like going to the restroom, and her breath should not be like its smell. Rather, it should be in such a way that the husband is eager and desirous without any compulsion to kiss his wife like a bunch of flowers and that however much he kisses her, his desire increases so that he kisses her again. These considerations play a role when the wife has bad breath, and to silence the husband she says, "You don't like me! If you did, as they say:

"The smell of onions from the mouth of the loved one
Smells better than a flower from the hand of a beldam."[63]

She tries to cover her bad breath with stupid apologies, which is a lame excuse. The poor man has to endure this and says, "Yes, yes." One should teach such women. But if God has not afflicted her with bad breath, an ugly face, or an unbecoming appearance, she should not eat bad-smelling things or she should not make her beautiful face ugly.

It is obvious that when someone gets up from sleep, there are some changes in her face and in her breath. Just by washing her face, brushing her teeth, putting on a clean dress, and applying makeup, she makes everything proper. It is stupid and not fair not to do so. There is no excuse for not doing these things, unless it is out of stupidity and ignorance. If a woman does not understand this, she should not expect to be a beloved, and she should go her own way.

If the ladies want me to express the manners and etiquette for women, it would be a lengthy book, and this little treatise cannot contain all of it; I have said one-thousandth of it very briefly in this book.

Unfortunately, whoever of these respected ladies looks at it will do nothing but curse me because as the Prophet of God has said, "The truth is bitter." You cannot say the truth to the wise men of the nation, let alone to women, who have half the intelligence of a man. They will say, "By God, you stupid man, as if you have nothing else to do," and "God grant you better inspiration," and "Go, you stupid man, if you are out of work, may God give you subsistence from another place! If you are saying the truth, go and write a book for men," or "Give this advice to your own wives." If God grants them a little bit of fairness and they look at this book dispassionately, they will know that I am saying the truth, and they will not harvest bad fruit from it. If they send their daughters to school, they should put this book into their hands on the first day and should recommend them to read it and act accordingly. Then their daughters will not be as distressed as their parents are.

I have said whatever I had in my mind;
Heed it or despair, however you're inclined.[64]

The book *Education of Women* was finished on Saturday, Sha'ban 5, 1304, by the hands of this copyist, Mohammad Mehdi Golpeygani.

PART TWO

The Vices of Men

Introduction

First, from the beginning I praise God, who created women from the left rib of man. In the beginning of the year 1312 *hijri* [1894–95], which coincides with the forty-eighth anniversary of the auspicious reign of His Majesty the Shadow of God in Tehran, which is the capital of his most fortunate and sagacious majesty Naser al-Din Shah, may his reign be eternal, one day one of this humble author's closest friends delighted me with her presence in my humble abode. She found me wasting my time on this book. Although it may not be of any importance, she found it of utmost interest and asked me to write a chapter about my ancestors and what professions they had been engaged in. Having been given this task, I had no choice but to write this short account. Because I did not have much knowledge of some of the details, I therefore took them from the chronicles of the illustrious Qajar government.

This humble author is the daughter of the late Mohammad Baqer Khan, the commander of the Astarabad cavalry, who was one of the loyal servants of this powerful and victorious government. In the wars with the Turkmen, his services were known and evident to all government leaders. After fifty years of service, he was martyred while executing his services. My grandfather was the late Karbala'i Baqer Khan, the *qollar-aghasi* of the late king, may his soul rest in peace. In the days when the king [Fath 'Ali Shah] was heir apparent and governor of Fars, he was of service to him, and once, during the hunt,

57

he cut a lion into two with his sword in front of the shah, and the sound of "bravo" was echoed from the Leo of heaven. After sixty years of service, he was martyred in the war with Fathi Khan.[1] The late shah bought his severed head for one thousand *tuman*s, put it with his body, and buried him. My other grandfather, the late Hamzeh Khan, from the time of the late shah until the beginning of the reign of the current shah, was employed in government service in the border area of Astarabad. All his services are known to His Majesty. All great services that he has performed in Torshiz and Goklen[2] and other parts have been recorded in the Qajar chronicles, and there is no need for further description. My mother is the daughter of the late Akhund Molla Kazem, a *mojtahed* from Mazandaran, residing in Barforush, may God elevate his stature. He was an outstanding master in many sciences, and for fifty years he was busy teaching sciences and dispensing justice in the religious courts in the capital of Tehran. After his death, my mother was employed in the royal harem for thirty years in the service of Her Highness Shekuh al-Saltaneh, the mother of the heir apparent. She made several journeys to Azerbaijan and for several years was in the service of His Highness the crown prince; now she resides in the holy places [Karbala and Najaf] and is engaged in prayer for the preservation of the royal family.

In short, this humble author did not consider herself able to educate men; therefore, I wrote *The Vices of Men* in answer to *The Education of Women* so that men's failings would be known. Perhaps they now will refrain from educating women and devote themselves to their own education. I do so in four chapters, including their manner of treating women, and then discuss their own behavior. The first chapter is about the manner of drinkers of wine. The second chapter is about the manners of the gamblers. The third chapter contains a description of the users of opium, bhang, the pipe,[3] and hashish.[4] The fourth chapter is a discussion of rowdies, cutthroats, sodomites, and perverts.[5]

The target of this humble author is those men who are of low morals because it is obvious that such behavior and comportment cannot come from wise, intelligent, and capable men. So these characteristics are owing to a lack of intelligence and understanding in those people, who are even lower than animals of burden and more dangerous than wild animals, and God Almighty has truly said about them, "They are lower than cattle, nay even worse."[6] An intimate and confidante of His Majesty, Mohammad Ebrahim Khan, known as Khalvati, has written a long, pleasant, and eloquent account about such deceitful people in his book *Adab-e Naseri* (Naserean Manners), and he has also called them the lowest of low.[7] But since the present book was written by my sisters' wish, I wrote a few words in the manner of advice so that my sisters in religion may benefit, and I hope that they will remember me in their prayers.

Advice to Women with the Help of God

"My greetings to accomplished ladies and young maidens so that they be aware and accept advice, so that salvation will be yours in this world and the world to come."

God Almighty has created you women for men so that you will be as a harvest for them and to increase progeny; otherwise, no other work is expected from you. Think about it: Do you have such penetrating wisdom to accomplish great works, or do you have strength and prowess to be equal to your enemies, or do you have so much capability that you can earn your living by your own sweat, or, without the hindrance of women's monthly period, are you able to pray in purity for forty days to God Almighty? So you are a feeble female, deficient in everything; you should be obedient to your husband's orders and never go out of the house without his permission and not to show your ornaments to a strange man. You should be all smiles to your husband, and even if you die of hunger, you should not ask anything from him. Whatever dress he buys for you, you should put it on, not throw it away, and not show displeasure. In play and love, you should be bold. In fight and strife, you should be silent. Do not tell anybody his secrets; you should not want to destroy and defame him. Do not make lying, cheating, or deceiving a habit of yours. You should not give your husband's property to anyone, and if you have any property of your own, you should not begrudge him.

But, my sisters in religion, you should fulfill all these admonitions provided the husband be faithful, fears God, avoids sin, and behaves kindly and well toward his wife. He should not ask her something that cannot be done, and he should not find fault and quibble with you. He should not be ruthless and cruel; he should also not be stubborn and always with his friends and a truant from home; he should not womanize and be loving boys or, like a spineless husband, divorce his wife without any reason. If the husband has any of these traits, then, of course, it is much better that you get rid of him as soon as possible while you are young and not burdened with sons and daughters.

> Do not behave in a way that misery weighs you down
> Now that you have the means get rid of that frown.[8]

In the name of God, the Merciful and the Compassionate.

We are servants of a God and worshippers of a creator who has brought forth beautiful flowers from the earth and placed arousing wine of love in their hearts to adorn the meadows and give comfort to friends. He has made the nightingales disclosers of the secrets of the gardens and the turtledoves preachers of the meadows, the owls settlers of the ruins and partridges lodgers in the mountains.

> All the firmament under your banner stands
> Our existence depends on you, your being by itself stands.[9]

Praise God and salutations to the Prophet[10] and his saintly descendents and their holy ancestors, may peace be upon all of them, who are guides of the road and saviors in the pass of errors, to continue: one day I was in the house of a friend, where there was a gathering of women, and the meeting became very lively. This humble author was the garden's nightingale and the singing bird of the congregation. Each story had a moral, and each tale an advice, so much so that we ended up gossiping, and I tried to stop them. I said the Prophet has said, "Gossiping is worse than adultery." One of the women who had a sallow face and a heart full of sorrows because of her unmanly husband sighed deeply and said, "Oh my sister, you do not know anything of our grieving and burning hearts. You consider this unburdening of sorrows as gossip."

> One who has not seen our beloved
> Is not aware of our affairs.

I replied, "If I am not aware of your affairs, I am fully cognizant of my own. Whatever you complain about is your right." When I said this, they all got together, and they all insisted asking, "What is happening to you?" I said, "My story will take books to fill. Words fail to do right by my eagerness." They said, "By God, we will not let you go until you have given a full account of your affairs." When they said this, I had no choice but to tell them what has happened to me. I said, "My dear friend became a snake in my bosom, my house became a cave, and my bright day became a dark night." They were amazed, and their interest increased because I had never complained of my husband, and, unlike my sisters, I had always praised his good qualities. I was content and pleased with him. If sometimes someone complained of her husband, I would reproach her, saying that this is the way of error because the fault is in us, not in the men. We are feeble of intellect, weak in faith, whereas they are perfect in creation. If a human being cannot see something openly, experience it, sense the difficulty, and not suffer the hardship of this treacherous world, she will not be wise and able to take advice. This humble author, because I was without experience and naive, would not inquire about certain affairs, for as the poet says:

Description of this separation and sorrow
Leave this time for another tomorrow.[11]

The story and the affairs of my life will be related, not in short, but in detail, to my heart-grieving and tearful sisters.

How can you hide tinder in a cotton ball?
However much you try, it will become a fireball.

I have a hidden grief in my heart, and my heart is perturbed by sorrow. One of the sisters said:

Hear another story of the tricks of fate
A story full of grief and fright, I tell it straight.

"And it is a book written by a rascal, who is unique and a wonder in the world. He has given it the inauspicious name *The Education of Women*. I have seen it, and it is ready here. Have a look at it."

When I perused these pages, I found out that the author believes himself to be educated and wants to be the educator of women. He has put together a nonsensical argument, which has no base and in its utmost tastelessness has taken a stubborn route and with its biting tongue has decided to cut the roots of women. Even worse, he has made it into ten chapters and in each chapter has put forward an unrealistic criticism, senseless and more biting than the thorn of a thistle aimed at women. I did not like the book; I threw it aside, and in my mind I was debating and deliberating plans how to answer him. Although I did not have this intention, I eventually decided to make an effort, and in good rhyming Persian like a flowing stream I wrote a book in answer to this evil-natured man so that men would know that among women there are still those who are of high standing and whose force of speech may benefit from their eloquence. How nicely has Sheikh Sa'di said it:

> O intelligent man, what is the tongue in the mouth?
> It is the key to the treasure door of a virtuous man.
> When the door is closed how can one know
> Whether he is a seller of jewels or a hawker?[12]

Although according to logic, reason, and the verses of the Koran men are above women, and God has said, "Men are the protectors and maintainers of women,"[13] not every man is better than every woman, and not every woman is less than every man. Maryam,[14] Zahra,[15] Asiyeh,[16] and the great Khadijeh are women, whereas Pharao, Haman,[17] Shemr,[18] and Senan[19] are men.

> Not everyone who puts his hat aslant and arrogantly sits
> Knows the way of ruling and kingship.[20]
> Take a guide, one who goes straight, be it a female
> Because when Khedhr is lost in the dark, his mare guides
>   his trail.

All the affairs of this lowly world are relative and additions.

It is enough for women that even when men are elevated to the highest ranks, nevertheless they are borne of women and coming out of them.

Oh earthly body, whether you are noble or base
You are earth born and issue of the elements.[21]

As it was said, the author of this book seems to have made his own taste a guide for himself. He does not know that tastes[22] differ inordinately, and each one has different ways; everybody's nature is the opposite of the other, and each man is of a different disposition. Each person wants a woman and a life of his own that others do not like. As it will become clear in this writing and its criticisms, each issue will be fully explained because in that gathering of my sisters they heard my words and liked them very much. They asked me emphatically to write them down. In asking me to write them, they insisted excessively, so per force I started preparing the book answering the criticisms of the book *The Education of Women,* wrote for each a satisfying answer, and made my sisters happy and pleased. I call this composition *The Vices of Men* and hope that by the will of God and his blessings men will not go around repeating these evil doings and sayings.

First, one of the statements of the author is that girls say we will not become the wives of turbaned, long-robed, and long-bearded men who ignore justice, do not listen to music, or to those who are of a perturbed disposition, ill tempered, and poor. He considers this a failing of those poor girls and has criticized them excessively, saying words that are worse than any curse. Now, let us look fairly at the whole matter to see whether the girls are right or not because life and happiness for these young maidens with such men, particularly with the old ones, how can it be? Especially when the girls by upbringing and status do not have anything in common with them, in particular when they may be daughters of military men or literary men, children of nobility or daughters of respectable merchants; each one of those has no affinity whatsoever with [these men] because similar upbringing and social status are of the highest importance in marriage.

Birds of a feather flock together.

At this time, when evil characteristics have rendered Iranians worse than animals, most of those characteristics are present in men, and they have lost their good traits. So, therefore, this matter shows the good taste and intelligence of the girls, not their faults and shortcomings, unless they are children of the same type of men who would be of the same social origin and class. In that case, similar words will not be heard from those girls because, on the contrary, they will not be asking for people who are unlike them. As it has been seen many, many times and evidenced by experience, there is no need for reasoning and proof because compatibility in upbringing is natural, and attachment to everything by nature comes by the passage of time, and these are obvious to the intelligent.

End of the introduction.

Chapter One

In the first chapter [of *The Education of Women*], the author has said that if a man takes the hand of his wife and wants to put it into the fire, that wife should obey him, be quiet and silent, and show no resistance. Oh my God, Mowlana, with such an intelligence and understanding, if you had not composed this book, what would have happened? There are many deceitful and ill-natured men who, out of evil intention, search and find a woman with property to marry her. Thereafter, by hook and crook, by deceit and tyranny, or with pleasant and unpleasant manners, he gets hold of her property. He madly squanders the property as if it were stolen money, on ridiculous expenditures such as alchemy, gambling, whoring, pederasty, and parties. Then he falls into misery, poverty, and begging and will divorce that poor woman with or without children. Then he will go after another woman. Such faithless men can be found by the thousands in this time of ours. All the religious, customary, provincial, municipal, and village courts have been involved in such cases for many years, and they still are. You lowly wretch who have come of late to become a counselor to women, may it be that you are one of those devils, and with this device and deceit you have printed this book, making yourself their counselor so that they will end up in your trap. It is strange that this ignoramus, who considers himself one of those so-called westernized and civilized people and an imitator of European teachers, nevertheless clearly is not even half-civilized. All the people of Europe apparently consider the [following] verse as if it was like "the book of Mani and the drawings of Arzhang," and they consider it as a model.[23]

> Verily, women are like flowers that we have created for you and all of you desire the smell of flowers.[24]

You have to obey them, and there needs to be total faith and harmony, without a shadow of strife and discord between husband and wife, and women need to be respected more than men are. Unlike the people of Europe, this ill-mannered, faultfinding, unrefined author all the time seeks to humiliate women and tries to cover all their good qualities with imaginary and false failings. Curse be on you and your doings.[25]

5. The Moslem intellectual in Paris and his own town. From the journal *Molla Naser al-Din* 4, no. 4 (25 Jan. 1909).

Chapter Two

In the second chapter, he has said that with words, wounds are worse than sword cuts. This statement is true, one should not hide it; it has been well said: the wounds by swords heal, but the wounds afflicted by the tongue cannot heal.

> Words hurt a man much more
> Than a sword can hit his core.[26]

In truth, not in any time, not in any land has it happened that someone says, "May I be your sacrifice," and she answers, "Go to hell!" As long as the man does not hurt the wife a hundred times with his tongue and does not target the wife, she will not react in an ugly fashion.

> The answer to nonsense is more nonsense;
> Throw a clod and expect a stone as recompense.[27]

So far it has never happened that someone in return for good has written bad and in return of bad things has written and said positive things. In particular, women who sit at home behind closed doors are barred from all sorts of social interactions and from acquiring good manners and education. They associate with women and children who are deficient [in manners], with girls and women who are involved in daily work, the troubles and chores of taking care of the home and the children, and all these activities are never ending. In spite of all this, women, unless they have been tongue lashed repeatedly, they will not hurry to answer, and this fact does not remain hidden to the impartial, wise and just, although the author has denied it.

Chapter Three

The third chapter deals with the complaints of wives about men, which he considers a major failing because a wife should never complain about her husband, for someone else does not know whether the complaint is made out of love and affection, and nobody complains about a stranger, opponent, and enemy.

> If Leyla liked others so much,
> Why did she break my bowl?[28]

If men behaved friendly and caring from day one in the same way as they do during the time of the honeymoon and courting and did not change their words and manners, and

6. The child bride is being taken to her husband's house. From *Molla Naser al-Din* 1, no. 15 (14 July 1906).

they become accustomed to that behavior and acquire good manners, then they will not be confronted with ugly behavior. Because a wife has no choice but to be under the husband's control, apart from her husband she does not know, does not see, and does not associate with anybody else.

> I have no place of refuge but your threshold;
> In this world, my head cannot rest but in your fold.[29]

Chapter Four

In the fourth chapter, he discusses women's sulking. He considers this a failing, but if between man and wife there is affection, like between father and daughter, sulking won't be animosity but affection. To be coy and sulk is the best way of the beloveds, which tests the love of the husband at that moment. The author of the book has considered all women slaves and servants and all men as kings and masters. If there is the occasional talk of intercourse, it is considered a bodily function such as relieving oneself, which has nothing to do with lovemaking and enjoyment.

> You have neither love, chivalry, nor nobility.
> You poltroon of a man, where is your civility?

But it is not like this, and not all men are like this. Because the author does not have enough intelligence, it is better that he not be the educator of women. In God we take refuge, and we seek his aid [in such matters].

Chapter Five

Concerning how women should walk. A woman has to take small steps and talk softly and weakly like a person who has just risen from the sickbed. Of course, such a woman is good for a great emir, who is blood lusty, evil, tyrannical, and a faultfinder. All the housework and the work outside are done by men, and the wife stays at home; she has no children, no relatives, no day and night work, and all the time looks after the husband, and if the husband is pleasure loving, he seeks his pleasure outside the home. Or if she is the wife of a poor man, then in addition to her many burdensome and difficult chores she has to please him as well. How can she behave in this way, be like a humble slave in the service of the mighty master? God the Provider does not ask such a formidable task of his servants that this new educator of women asks of women. It seems that this man imagines that the whole world is like him, and in accordance with his own imagination he gives instructions to everyone. Well done! People are different, and their natures are different, and their tastes are opposites; in creation and nature, you cannot measure everyone with the same stick as if the law of religion has been changed and the law of civilization has been uprooted. Humanity and education have gone to the dogs, and suddenly somebody has appeared with imaginary thoughts that are against all the laws of nations. He has put together some nonsensical arguments, has no sources for them, calls them *The Education of Women,* and wants to educate women.

> What has not partaken of existence
> To others can never impart existence.[30]

If you are bent on criticizing women, their good points will turn into faults.

> If you talk, you are a loud timbal
> If you are quiet, you're but a picture on the wall
> If you wing like an angel to the sky,
> The ill wishers won't let you fly.[31]

But if one is just, fair, and loving, then

> You see seventy faults and one virtue
> But a friend gives only that one its due.[32]

Poor women are attacked from every side; poets satirize them, scholars and literary men make sarcastic remarks about them and call it advice; they are shameless. In such a time, which is obvious to any intelligent person, the book *Education of Women* appears, adding insult to injury.[33] May God hasten the day of deliverance and make the day of salvation near.

7. Eating at home from the tablecloth. From *Molla Naser al-Din* 2, no. 20 (1 June 1907).

Chapter Six

This chapter is about how women should eat. He has said that a woman should sit on her knees next to the tablecloth and eat delicately; she should not talk, make no sound, not answer anyone—meaning play pantomime—and eat with three fingers. Look at this fairly: if a woman with a few children sits like that at the tablecloth, would those children leave a single dish unturned, and would they give anyone occasion to eat? If a woman remains silent, those children will pour the bowl of sauce [*khoresh*] into the juice or the juice on top of the rice. If the wife does not say anything or goes forward and whispers in the ear of the child, "May Daddy become your sacrifice, be quiet, sit, and do not talk!" then the children will make life intolerable for her and her husband and ruin the food so that both husband and wife as well as the small children will go hungry and the dishes will be broken. Yes, if a man with his wife, in the manner of Europeans, goes to a hotel, perhaps they can behave according to his instructions. But in Europe, according to the travel and geography books, all women are respectable and educated, and they know many things, and they sit at the table with strangers, and at the time of dancing they take the hands of other men and dance. But the rules of the religion of Islam are different; all Iranian women are busy with housework and chores, especially the women of the common people. The author takes his own taste as an example and says that a wife should sit far from the husband. This is the same idea of service that he has dreamed up that I have mentioned before. Otherwise, love, affection, and the relations between lovers are totally different from what he says, and you cannot imagine them to be in this manner. May God give him some sense.

Chapter Seven

All of what he has said concerning cleanliness, makeup, jewelry, hygiene, perfuming, being pleasant, and the good nature of women is in accordance with the taste of the common people and the nobility—provided that all the means necessary are available and that there are no poverty and destitution, which cause uncleanliness, but rather that there are wealth and riches, which bring cleanliness and hygiene. The husband should love his wife, not be pederastic, faultfinding, coarse, and he should provide with care and out of love whatever the wife asks.

To the ill-natured and faultfinding husband, she should say:

Seeing the death angel is better than seeing you
May I be smitten by a scorpion rather than touched by
   you.[34]

It has been seen and heard many times that those men who have beautiful wives pay no attention to them and are always engaged in their debauchery. One of my relatives who has been helpful in writing this book has asked me to put this story here, and I have no responsibility for it. She has related that a man had a very beautiful wife in whom he was not interested. Every day he would find a new fault with her and would leave the women's quarters in anger and sleep elsewhere in the house. One night he asked a servant to go and find a boy for him. The poor servant went looking for a boy and searched everywhere, but he could not find one. He went to the house of a prostitute who had a handsome, shapely brother and asked for him. The sister said, "My brother has gone on a journey, but I am ready to go in his place." The poor servant said, "My master is a pederast and will not ask for you." The woman said: "I will dress like a boy and behave like one, so that he will not notice it and will reward you well." The servant agreed because he had no choice and he was greedy. The woman dressed as a boy and came to the house of the master. The man, as soon as he heard the door, came running on bare feet and embraced the boy-looking woman like a sweet soul, as if he were a boy from paradise. Out of passion and excitement, he did not even take off her clothes but threw her onto the bed face down. Because the woman was not accustomed to anal sex, her passage was tight, and the man therefore ordered her to be lubricated. The woman mistakenly thought the lubrication a good excuse and did not let go of his genitals. The man was pressing so hard that the servant watching through a keyhole almost died of eagerness. During the ups and downs of sexual intercourse, the man took her hand away in search of the boy's penis. After much trial, he found out that she was a woman and that the place of entrance was in front, not in the back. He got angry because his penis flagged and his sexual drive went away. He shouted, "You deceitful servant, what is this, who is this that you have brought?" The servant became flustered and said, "You can do it both ways, do not become frustrated. There is no need to become violent and be angry." He said, "But this is a woman!" The servant said, "Whatever the boy has, she also has." The master said, "She has no dick." The servant said, "In such a moment, what do you care for a prick?" The master said, "When I enter him from the back, I want to play with his dick." The servant said, "An anus is an anus, and a dick is a dick. Enter her from the back, and play with mine." The master started laughing so much that he fell down from the bed [which had been placed under a tree]. His penis was cut by a nail on the bed, and a branch of the tree tore his arse. He cried out and fell senseless. The prostitute and the poor servant had no choice but to flee, and they took whatever was precious in the house with them. A boy servant came and saw the master in that situation and ran back shouting and informed the lady. The lady came and, seeing the husband in that condition, tore her dress and wept bitterly. The neighbors came and brought a surgeon, a physician, and the master to his senses. The poor master was very remorseful for what he had done and with all these troubles and tribulations could not stay in his country, and he chose to go on a long journey. Such is the fate of most pederasts, womanizers, gamblers, and alchemists, and in this way they treat their women, and their wives treat them accordingly. Oh, people of intelligence, take heed.

Chapter Eight

Concerning women's clothes, he has said that if women put on long and large drawers and skullcaps with floral patterns, it is very pleasant. Again, he has chosen a way of showing his bad taste and stubbornness; it is as if these verses have been exactly written for this tasteless man:

> A striped, brocaded skullcap on your head
> Your long underwear too long and pleated
> You are my husband, worthless piece of shit,
> If nobody wants you, I do, come and get it.[35]

In short, each wife has to act according to her husband's taste and liking. Although many women act in accordance with their husbands' desire, yet because of their [choice of] dresses and jewelry they do not please their husbands. Many women buy soft, delicate, and expensive fabrics with their own money for themselves and their husbands; they cut them, sew them, wear them, and clothe the men. In spite of all this, the wretched husband does not care at all, and that poor woman is always despised and not appreciated by him. There is nothing that can serve as a condition for something else—that is, no reasoning can be said to be absolute, especially in this time when there is no order and rule. Everything needs to be discussed and agreed upon; therefore, nobody knows his duties; there is no unity, discord and divergence rule, sincerity and unity do not exist.

Chapter Nine

Concerning sleeping habits, what he has said is right, and there is no shortcoming in it. Again it depends on being wealthy, not poor, and the provisions of life being readily available in every aspect, unlike the situation for us, the poor and needy people of Iran, where for thirty years a couple sleeps under the same quilt from early night until morning with all sorts of unpleasant smells and strange sounds in between, during winter and summer. All this is the result of poverty and ignorance and nothing else. Otherwise, every intelligent being differentiates between good and bad, desirable and undesirable. There is no need for so much talk.

> What makes lion's actions turn into fox's deeds,
> It is nothing but need, need, and need.[36]

Of the other mannerisms, coquetry, and charm that a woman has to display in bed for her husband, the author has given a special description and detailed narration all to his own taste. At the same time, the taste of most men is contrary to his taste because they like other activities and coquetries. The wives of seminarians and mollas act differently, which is quite obvious to any intelligent and fair person as day is different from night. This is not the way of the "education" because there are different and various types of men and women, good and bad, both common and noble, and good and bad characteristics can be observed in everyone. If you want to educate them, you have to educate everyone. Education is dependent on all rules of civilization—that is, national, governmental, religious, civil societal, and military values. With these few words in no way can people be educated, and His Excellency, the writer of the book *The Education of Women,* has wasted much toil in vain.

Chapter Ten

Concerning women getting up in the morning, the writer has said that the wife, as soon as she gets up from bed, has to leave the husband to the slave girls and servants. It is obvious what is meant by this advice. As soon as the lady goes out of the room, the master feels up the slave girls and the servants and in this way enjoys himself. Now, let us look at this fairly. After the master behaves in this way with the servants, how can that poor lady keep order and discipline in her own house among that group of wild, unruly, and foolish people? The rules of housekeeping have gone out of the window, and living conditions become strained. As they say, "This is the day of ruination of the cities, and the torment of people will be apparent." If the lady says that the servants do not obey or that they are stealing, the master reacts that she says so out of a grudge. All this comes from being too familiar with the servants. What has been said so far concerns the good works of men; their bad works are countless—I take refuge in the anger of God.

It becomes evident that the bad women of this time are better than the bad men of this time because they are demure and forbidden from having association with men. By nature, they are less cruel and less evil because they are emotionally, physically, and intellectually weak, and disproportionate cruelty is foreign to them. If it happens, then it is all because of their husbands. Because husbands are the educators of women and women are captives in their hands,

8. Domestic scene. From the journal *Mazali* 2, no. 26 (27 June 1915).

and that is why so many vices have appeared. May God join them with their husband. Oh God, hasten the coming of our master, the master of our time, divine deputy and propagator of the Koran.

9. ". . . And tell them what you have said or done in the darkness." E. Powys Mathers, *The Education of Women*, London, 1927.

The Vices of Men

In the Name of God the Compassionate and Merciful.

This is the book called *The Vices of Men*.

We praise God, whose least endowment is the greatest gift to the inhabitants of the earth, and we are thankful to the Provider, whose lowest grace is the highest supplication of people of authority; as a result of accepting providence, some suffer, some become lovers, and some remain in the valley bewilderment. He made Eve companion to Adam and Zuleykha companion to Joseph; he made Farhad a distracted lover of Shirin, and Khosrow bewildered by Shakar. He made Joseph the beloved of Zuleykha and Majnun the beloved of Leyla. However, whatever we search, look for, and say is out of ignorance, and this is all right, for we are but human beings. His essence is free from questions and doubt and from what they say. Praise and salutations to the holy and shining soul of the best of creation.

> Ahmad, the prophet who is wisdom's fount,
> Both worlds are attached to his mount.

The holy Tradition about him says, "Was it not for you, we would not have created the firmament." After this penmanlike praise of God and all the prophets, hail from every side to his definite vice regent and the successor of the Prophet and his holy family, who contain all the best qualities and are devoid of any sin. But man in every time and at every moment should not

83

waste his precious life and good leisure time. He should follow the Tradition of the Holy Prophet in praying and offering humble salutations to God, in all cases be content with his provisions, and avoid the deceits and the cheats of the accursed Satan so that he will not end up in the well of ignominy. He should gradually efface the essence of ignorance from himself and not engage in foolishness, sin, and that which has been forbidden. He should kill the lust, keep his heart alive; he should suffer for the sake of people so that people will rest because of him.

> Worship of God is nothing but serving one's fellow men.[37]
> But not through rosary, prayer rug, or a dervish's robe you
>   can.

He should purify his mind of vain thoughts, rectify his character, and illuminate his essence with the light of perfection.

> Associate with the riders of the sun
> Seek your own trouble and your friends' fun.[38]

We don't mean a person who is crude inwardly and outwardly and is always evil intentioned, or one whose heart is deceitful and whose inner nature is full of intrigue, who is in ignorance master of Abu Jahl[39] and in rebelliousness a follower of Satan. He spends his time continuously in drinking or partaking of hemp dust [*chars*][40] and bhang without any consideration for his reputation. He fears neither man nor God. Out of deceit and malice, he sometimes pretends to people that he has reached heaven and has become a companion of Gabriel and Israfil.[41] He never walks on the path of sincerity and does not go along with the desires of his friends. He does not breathe except with malice; he does not go one step unless with evil intent. He spends his dear life in summer and winter in useless pursuit of beloveds, music, and wine in taverns or Armenian quarters, on which he spends day and night and wastes all of his time, and this ode in quintrains has been written for him:

These artless men	Ill-famed and vagrant
Useless is what they say	Harmful is what they do

Women suffer because of them

Night and day nothing but sin	God has seen from them
Religion and faith is ruined by them	a dead man is better than them

They are worse than scum

Debauchery and depravity is their job	Sin and vice is their way of life
Satan is their bosom friend	To the fair ones they are like a fiend

They are like pigs and asses

If they earn anything by their sweat	They shortchange the scales
They cheat and deceive without shame	And give themselves a bad name

From top to toe

God has said: if you marry	In the tradition of the Prophet
If you deny the rights of the wife	You are an infidel in your faith

You will end up in hell

If you know "Fearing not being fair"[42]	If for your family's sake "I do" you declare
If all other laws you denied	By those of women you should abide

Poor ignorant women

Not only do you deny women's rights	But all the time you increase their plight

You abuse your power and might   And beat them without respite
                Continuously day and night
All of you want gratification   But there is no appreciation
Owing to lack of any passion   You are useless and but an
                                    affliction
            Their situation is worse than bad
Ever without wisdom and   They are blind and lame
    acclaim
As to this tribe of ill-fame   God said: they're not the
                                    same . . .
        Animals are even better than them
Whoever is born vicious   In this world will not become
                                virtuous
Whoever is born auspicious   By nature will be righteous
            May we all be His sacrifice.

Drinking Party

At sunset, a group of vain-talking, vain-walking, dastardly
lowlifes come together, and because of their behavior everyone complains. They go to the Jew's house or to the Chris-
tian's tavern, and in the fashion of drinkers they get three
pennies of arrack and one penny worth of tripe; they come
out drunk and stupidly satisfied, shouting and singing. They
pass through some dreadful places, they make a display of
themselves by baring their breasts, and then God knows what
happens. But those who are great men, nobles, aristocrats,
emirs, ministers, and high-ranking officers, who are common
and worse than animals, gather in a special house of one of
the notables, which has been chosen for this party, and they
like this assembly to be as bright as a candle. Drinks and hard
liquor, of whatever is necessary, is ready: wine of Hamadan,

10. Drinking after the breaking of the fast during Ramazan. From *Molla Naser al-Din* 9, no. 23 (23 July 1914).

good wine from Isfahan, the best Khollar wine from Shiraz, date wine from Ahvaz, strong brandy from Ardabil, mastic arrack, ginger rum, brandy, 40 percent proof arrack from Marand, champagne, Bordeaux and Spanish cognac, from wherever it can be obtained. Whatever makes you drunk, they get it and drink it, and they eat stuff ranging from snacks to kebabs, well-prepared dried fruits, and selected pickles, of birds whatever they desire—partridge, francolin, turkey, yellow partridge, quail, pheasant, caponized cock—as well as roasted trout, and with various melodious musical instruments such as the harp, the violinette [*kamancheh*], the rebec, the lute, and the flute at the lips and the drum in the hands they make music. In the first round, the drinkers and singers' heads become heated, and their eyes and faces lose their shame, and they sing.

> On one side, music makes passionate commotion
> On the other, the jug of wine beckons to action
> On one side, what blossoms of wine on the lips appears
> On the other, a kebab skewer makes my eyes full of tears
> On one side, the lute and drum make a passionate
>   harmony
> On the other, the best of beloveds awaits your company.

In the midst of this, whoever is a little bit mad gets excited in the second round and starts swearing, and he considers this a pleasant way of acting. First, he turns to the owner of the house and says, "You pimp, smoke less of it, give it to me; do not be so cheap, so absolutely drunk; show some hospitality." The friend who is sitting next to him has loosened his suspenders, bared his head, and comfortably sits down on his rear end and says: "The son-of-bitch is drunk, talking nonsense." Another one comes in and says, "One is not less than the other; both shits are drunk."

> The wine with dregs makes them supine.
> What would happen if it were pure wine?[43]

Things gradually get out of hand, altercations start, squabbles ensue, and tempers run high.

One got mad and swore,
He immediately replied with more
And called the other "a half-wit"
While he called him "a pure shit."
In short, from talking to swearing
The uproar ended in fighting.

Those who were sitting rise up, and those who were already up are already fighting. The ruckus moves from inside to outside in the garden, and club wielders come in. Hands grab daggers, and swords come out, and they take up flower stands and crack them on each other's head. Some are moaning, others lying with drawers down; some start running; some wounded and moaning with broken hands and heads are fleeing, saying: "What shall we do?" The author says:

Worried and in disarray	With torn arse, head not okay
This one blooded in the fray	The other fleeing away
One dying, the other faraway	

Having lost his wit	The other tore his outfit
Drunk with wine, on the fritz	The other has enough of this blitz
At that moment, he is less than an ass	
Spit on them and slime	Whoever from the wise
Curses blame them all the time	Will earn a grateful prize
From God who brings day and night	

One, vomiting, falls down; another, crying, falls on his face; another in the toilet empties his bladder. Then the news reaches the greedy, bare-feet police, who are worse than Iblis, and they pour forth from the door and the wall and come from every crevice and hole. They break the hands and feet of one, and they torture the others and drag them all to the police station. In spite of all this ruckus and crying, a few who have drunk less and still have some wits about them intercede with the police, saying, "Do not shame them, and get out of the house; whatever is needed will be paid. Tomorrow we will recompense you." The police say, "By God, it has past that stage. The report has gone to H.E.; your secret has come out into the open so that it cannot be mended. There is no alternative but to take you in, beat you up, imprison and fine you." These wretches of drunks who were interceding say, however, as the saying goes, "Foul was my speech; it has made my mouth so foul, as if I had eaten of filth itself, but it was my drunkenness that spoke, not I."[44]

Finally, after giving the inspector a sum, they are released. Those who are able go home, but in what manner? Their clothes are undone; heads and hands broken; they are bloodied, moaning, and limping. On the other hand, the poor wife of that low spineless bastard has been waiting hungry from evening till morning on the roof, while the food has gone cold, and nobody has partaken from it. The master comes and knocks at the door. The lady runs barefoot and opens the door, and what a sight she beholds. The husband is quite a spectacle. He yells, moans, and gives himself airs. He stumbles from one wall into the other, falling, rising, and sometimes not even able to rise. The lady, with the help of the servants, drags him into his bed and puts his head on the pillow. The lady and the poor servants eat the food that has been ruined and has become cold and bitterer than bitter gourd. They eat it and go to sleep. In the morning, after sunrise when the time of prayer has long past, he wakes up as if from the sleep of death. The poor lady prepares whatever is customary for him to eat every day, but this spineless husband with his sallow, grimacing face, when he enters makes such a fuss so that the events of last night will not be mentioned. That is, until he wants to go out, then the lady says, "We do not have any household money, can you give us some?" The master angrily bursts out, "I gave you money three days ago. How can I give more? Whatever I gave you, you took and spent on yourself, or you saved it. I have not more than this." The lady, seeing that it is no use and talk will only end up in fighting and being beaten up, perforce shuts up. The master leaves the house and on the way meets some friends, and each of them tells the other his news. Each asks about the other, and each one responds. One of them says, "In one of the houses of one of our friends and brothers, there is a gambling party. If you want we can go there and have fun for a while." Everyone agrees to go to there.

The Gambling Party

The second party is a gambling one. Friends come together at a friend's house. They knock on the door; the master of the house comes and opens the door, and with an open and smiling face he greets them. They all know that, as the saying goes, "the greeting of a peasant is not without expectation" because he will cheat and fleece them as much as he can. He says to the friends in a friendly, suave, and inviting voice, "Come forward; you are welcome; this house is yours, I am totally at your service." The friends, seeing that the master of the house is friendly, inviting, and sweet voiced, step inside completely at ease and careless. After having taken a seat, they say, "Dear brother, last night was a disaster for us, and we

11. "Wait a moment while I say my prayers!" From *Molla Naser al-Din* 4, no. 22 (31 May 1909).

are expecting you to put a guard at the door so that we will be at ease." The master of the house says, "Nobody has the right to enter the house without my permission. Be assured and do not worry about anything and start gambling because we have chess, backgammon, *as, teren, ganjefeh,*[45] and other games."

Chess is difficult because it needs two players and a separate room. Backgammon is difficult because winning depends on a good throw. As the saying goes, "Throwing a lucky dice makes everyone a good player." Then this apelike crowd sits down and starts playing *as.* One group sits down and starts playing *teren,* and another starts playing *ganjefeh,* and they get so busy that until the dusk they won't even eat or go to the toilet. If per chance somebody comes from somebody else's house and says [to that person], "Your father has died," he will say, "Leave the body in the house for the moment." If somebody [comes and] says [to somebody else there], "Your boss has sent for you," he will say, "Tell him, 'He is so sick that he will die soon.'" If somebody says [to one of them], "Your creditor is at the door," he will say, "He is an ass. Tell him to wait; God willing, tomorrow I will pay him in full if my hand wins." And if somebody says [to one of them], "Your wife has given birth to a son, and there is no butter [to grease her teats]," he will say, "May God make his coming felicitous. Tomorrow milk will come to her breasts." In short, their vices are countless.

Now we go to explain their game. One says, "Who is the bank?" The host says: "Do not bother yourself; whatever you want, I will have it ready in a moment." While they are discussing this, the gun is fired announcing the time of noon prayer. The host invites them to lunch, the friends hurriedly eat cheese and bread, and they hurry back to the game. Toward the evening, one of them who is somewhat religious says, "Friends, time of prayer is passing, so let's get up for the evening prayer." One who is losing shouts, "Deal the cards!

I have lost! I will not leave and lose my money." At any rate, the company continues playing until three hours into the evening. The host prepares dinner and says, "Please, come, eat and drink and then continue playing." Again, as at lunch, they eat something hurriedly, and instead of washing their hands, they wipe them off and continue gambling until morning and the time of prayer.

This one says: "I bid two cents."

The other says: "I won two dimes."

When true dawn shines upon this false group, because the sun is about to rise, this quasi-religious hypocrite once again shouts: "Friends, hurry, let's pray." He who was losing looks at his cards, sees four queens, and says, "Brother, do not talk nonsense, I have not come to pray." I see another look at his hand, and he sees four kings and says, "I'll raise you ten." The one who was urging them to pray looks at his hand and sees that he has four aces and forgets about prayer. He says, "I'll raise you twenty." In short, the players raise the stakes; the player with the four aces increases his bid, and whatever cash the friends had on the table he takes and goes away, and the friends are left bewildered and astonished. One of them says, "Friends, our first ancestor, Adam, did not have a watch." Another one joins in: "He did not have a robe and a jacket either." A third one says: "He did not have a hat and an overcoat." In short, whatever clothes and other accessories the friends had one of them has taken away and has departed, and they are left naked and lost. This is why the holy Koran says: "Oh you who believe, intoxicants and gambling and altars of idols and the games of chance are abominations of the devil; you should avoid them that you may succeed."[46] Truly, the word of God is the word of kings and the king of words.

Now we will relate one incident so that you may compare it to the rest. One of those who had absolutely lost everything was drunk and sleepy and went to his wretched house. He is sitting in a room, lost in thought, and imagining that if he would have had four aces, he would have won. Then he thinks, "My luck did not come, or perhaps the opponent cheated; otherwise, I was playing very carefully. And now, to redress the situation and recompense the time lost, I will go and sell some of the furniture of the house. I will drink a little bit of wine and put the rest of the money in the game so that my luck may turn so as to recover whatever I have lost." Following this line of thought, he gets up, and whatever his wife has of gold and jewelry in her box he takes and goes out. In the courtyard, the wife gets wind of it, comes and greets him, saying, "My darling sir, where were you last night, and where are you going now?" He says: "Woman, what is it to you where I go?" She says, "Then give us some money because for the last few days I have been borrowing, and nobody will lend me any more. After all, this is not the way you should treat your wife; this is not the way of being a husband." Hearing what his wife says, he cuffs her so hard that her mouth is bleeding and her teeth are broken. The wife, screaming and moaning, weeps, and that wretch of a man takes a club and beats his wife, driving her away from the house. On his way, he runs into a friend who all his life has been associating with drug addicts and lowlifes, and he sticks to him like gum and an ill-omened star, saying: "My dear friend, where have you been, and where are you going?" Whatever excuse he uses, it is of no use, so he per force goes with him, saying, "I had a thought, but it did not come true, so wherever fate takes me, I will follow." As the saying goes,

"In the Sufi path, whatever befalls the wayfarer is fine." They take each other's hand and walk in the street until they reach the house of that new friend, and they enter. A group of dervishes and some of those lowlifes get wind of their intention and gather there.

Hemp Dust, Bhang, and Opium Party

The third party concerns hemp dust, bhang, and opium. Those groups of addicts, who are worse than priests, start drinking, become high, and attempt to attain spiritual heights. One of them, tall as a spear, gets up, starts walking up and down, and says, "We poor dervishes are content with a smoke, which is out of this world. I want a real man who will take some cash from his pocket and spend it on us so that we can travel on our path and indulge in our imagination." Each of the friends throws down some money.

> Everyone liked this affair,
> Deeming it the best option for loving care.

One of them, who is the master of the group and servant of the dervishes, gathers the money. Hemp dust and bhang, which was not provided, is made ready. Opium and food are also prepared. The friends start smoking, and they eat and smoke until, as they say, "they become absolutely high." The heads of the happy dervishes, drinkers of bhang, smokers of the water pipe and hemp dust, eaters of opium are rolling, and their eyes are wide open, and they have vain dreams. One makes an ascension; another one reaches the moon or higher. Another one imagines himself to be in heaven, associating with the houris. Yet another one mistakenly believes he is a fortunate king on the throne, and the fifth one is thinking of a ministry and premiership. The sixth is falsely thinking himself to be a great agricultural entrepreneur, and all consider these hallucinations to be real and call them reality.

> A single thought caused their war and peace
> A single thought made their honor and dishonor.[47]

They spend their dear life and precious time with this kind of nonsense, absurdity, and evil acts in dens of iniquity. Oh wretch, what is the value of this world, let alone these hallucinations that you indulge in? You are disturbed because you are not getting it. I have heard that when Lokman the Sage was on his deathbed, he told his son: "After I am gone, bad friends will take you to be engaged in evil acts and debauchery; beware because they will deprive you of the benefits of this world and the good fortune of the world to come. One who is intelligent and is adorned with the ornament of sagacity is not going to be led astray by their fine words. Their companionship is like a poisonous snake, as the poet has said:

> "'Oh brother, evil company do forsake
> Bad friends will be worse than an evil snake
> The evil snake stings your body whole
> The evil friend harms your body and soul.'[48]

"But carnal nature man is eager for every kind of evil and forbidden acts, as the saying goes: 'Man is eager to do whatever is forbidden.' You are young, and it is normal for youth to do so. I beg you first, if you are inclined to do so, look at this party of your friends and see how it will end in ruination. If you accept this, then you are free, and if you want to gamble, gamble with Leylaj, who is the master of all gamblers. If you want to go whoring, see the whores first thing in the early morning, when they get up from sleep."

The son, after his father's death, was busy with mourning and grieving until the time of seeing his friends again arrived. He would go every day to see one of his friends. One night in the house of an intimate friend and a true companion, there was talk of a drinking party. They insisted and put pressure on him. The naive boy had no alternative but to drink. Meanwhile, he recalled the advice of his father, and, turning to his friends, he said, "You know I have never tried such untoward things and evil acts; you will be busy tonight until tomorrow, and I will learn, and gradually I will join you." In order to encourage him, they consented and became busy themselves. The first round passed in silence, the second with some commotion, and the third and fourth with burning hearts and with faces aflame. Whatever he had inside him, he expressed.

> Wine not only creates evil of every kind
> It reinforces whatever is in the mind.[49]

Those who had a somewhat good voice accompanied the singers, and those who knew how to dance joined the dancers and began to whirl and dance. The voices of those who were aggressive sounded like the braying of donkeys, and they began swearing and talking nonsense. One of them opposed him, some came to intervene; the result was altercation and fighting, and finally it ended up in beating with clubs and being wounded. The son, witnessing this, praised his father's soul and, remembering all other advice by his father, took his head between his hands and ran away. He said it is better to go to someone who is a master gambler. He looked for him, and they showed him a man who was staying in the stoking place of the bathhouse. He went to him and saw that he was up to his waist in the ashes, and the master gambler said, "Throw the sheep knuckles to the roof." He threw them up. He said, "Friend, go and see. It's a pair." When he went, he saw that the gambler was right. He turned back and said, "You are a master gambler, why are you so naked and wretched?" He said: "In gambling, even winning is a loss." The boy was confused and blessed his father's memory, and then he thought to himself that he should get some knowledge about prostitutes. Early in the morning, after prayer, he went to the brothel. By chance, he had a friend living nearby, and he reached his house. He knocked at the door, and the friend opened. After the usual greetings, the son made his intention known. The friend took him to the roof of his house and showed him all the prostitutes. It was the time that they got up from bed; they had not beautified themselves, and they showed themselves with foul-smelling mouths [and] disheveled hair, with sleepy red eyes and sallow grimacing faces, with a hangover from last night and a headache, as the poet has said:

> That vinegary grimace that is on your face,
> Even if it turns to honey, no fly will make it its place.

The son got so annoyed that he did not want to look again, came down from the roof, and left the house. On the way, he met a dervishlike friend who asked him, "Where are you going, master?" He said: "I am going home." He said, "You have to come to my humble abode and honor it with your presence." The man accepted it, and then both went to the friend's house. The son saw that two other men were there, and the host got up and prepared some hemp dust. He lit the head of the water pipe, put some hemp dust there, offered it to his guest, and said, "Brother, come and take a puff." The son said, "Give it to the other two gentlemen so that I can observe them, and if it is good, I will partake of it as well." The man readily accepted and smoked the water pipe and coughed profusely.

In no time, they became absolutely high and got into their own world. The son saw one of them was sitting on his knees and making complimentary remarks continuously, and he saw the other extending his hand as if he were gathering something and then hiding it in his underwear. A third one had put his head on the ground, raising his arse, and was continuously saying, "Hold me, I am falling." The son was bewildered by this behavior, and after they regained their consciousness, he asked them to explain what they had seen. The one who had been making complimentary remarks said: "After smoking, I saw I was sitting at a stream, and a molla was passing by, and I was greeting him." The second one said: "After becoming high, I was sitting in a big assembly of nobles and great men, and my flesh was continuously coming out of my drawers; I was having an erection, and I was trying to hide it so that I would not be ashamed in front of them." The third one said: "I was hallucinating and saw an angel taking me to heaven. She said, 'Let us go.' I said, 'I cannot fly.' She said, 'I will take you.' She put her finger in my arse and lifted me to heaven, and an archangel saw us and said, 'This is a debaucher. Why have you brought him here? You will be punished.' The angel who had taken me became afraid and was going to drop me, and I was saying, 'Do not take you finger out, and don't let go of me!'"

The son became astounded about what kind of joys these witless people had. They were neglectful of the affairs of both this world and the world to come. He recalled the counsel of his dear father and praised him much.

> To be worthy of receiving Grace, pure the seed must be
> Otherwise neither stone, clod, pearl, nor cornelian can be.[50]

Of these people who lost their way, it has been heard often that they have endangered themselves and have thrown themselves from heights and done most ridiculous things.

There is a story that one day a man bought some hemp dust from a grocer. He went to the public bath and used some hair remover on his body, and then suddenly he thought, "Why has not this stuff made me high?" and he came out of the bath naked and with hair remover all over him and went to the grocer and said: "Sir, why does your hemp dust have no effect? You have cheated me." The grocer laughed and laughed and asked the people, "O people, can you see if my hemp dust has any effect or not?"

At any rate, what was I saying, and what was I talking about? I was talking about the failings of man; I left the friends at the party of the opium eaters. They had taken hemp dust, and all fear had left them.

> Serenity was abandoned when it was time for opiates;
> Reason put aside respect for the Holy Faith or saints.

But this kind opium eating, which is called in their own lingo *vafur,* is worse than all other kinds. The only good thing about it is that it diminishes lust. That is why most women do not like an opium-eating husband. The major drawback of it is that if the man does not get it on time, he might suffer and even die. Using two grains of it, you can smoke as much as you like. Some who smoke and do not become high use opium juice,[51] and they take it from the soot[52] of opium in this way; they put it into a pot, let it boil, and then stick it into the *vafur* pipe [hookah]; they light it, and they put their head on a pillow and smoke it. The pleasure of this pipe is greater, but the ill effect is also greater. These people are worse than anyone and more wretched than anyone, and there is no sign of passion and manliness in them. They are sallow faced, ill tempered, faultfinding, and all evil characteristics are present in them.

> The toilet's corner is the addicts' hole
> There are tongs, skewers, grills, and coal
> Two in that claw and two in that talon
> One between the teeth like a roaring lion.[53]

The Party of the Libertines and Debauchers

The fourth party is that of the libertines and debauchers and a description of their lingo. They consist of different groups and display various behaviors; in them, there is no trace of passion or manliness, for malice and evil intent are in their nature. It is a group that is dauntless and careless, talking nonsense and vain words, being aggressive and violent, finding fault, pimping and snooping, pandering; they are drug addicts and greedy scoundrels, dirty gigolos, idlers and profligates; they all are scum and even worse. Some of them are soldiers, some are police officers, some are masons, some are tough guys, and some work for their livelihood. Those who are unemployed are debauched libertines.

Some of them find a poor son of a tradesman who is seeking pleasure and make friends with him, or, in their parlance, he is their "mark." What this poor character finds is that he is paying for these tarantulas and scorpions. Their house of pleasure and empty talk is the coffeehouse, where they sit on the platform, with their feet up, having no regard for rank and standing. By God, they know neither God nor the Prophet. The absurd and silly stories that they tell are full of nonsense, exaggeration, and lies. One says, "By the girdle of Horr,[54] by the shrine of 'Ali, when I became entangled in love of Khavar, the mustachioed prostitute, my love was so strong that I was the talk of town. So much so that every scoundrel [*mashti*][55] in the city and my friends had heard of me. Whatever I found, I spent on that mindless beloved to satisfy my unsatiated desires. That good-for-nothing eventually left me and became the beloved of 'Abbas Dash 'Ali." Another guy comes and says, "Brother, may your beard be bloodied and your moustache in my arse. I have spent more than you; I suffered more than you, and I could not take pleasure at all. For six months, I was after the son of Ja'far-e Lokhti [Ja'far the Naked]; I could not talk to him but with a thousand troubles. I was preparing the ground so that one night I might sleep with him. I just wanted to rip the curtain of his chastity, to bare his bum, to get my heart's desire, when suddenly Hasan Baqer Aqa woke up and got wind of our affair, and I said:

"'When my raw morsel was cooked and well done,
Hot from my mouth you took it, and it was gone.'[56]

"After that night, that good-for-nothing boy never got back to me."

Another of the *mashti*s says: "Brothers, do not think that you are the only ones who spent your money to no avail." He then sings this song:

"The *mashti*s you see all are poor as a church mouse
I have a better twofold shirt at my house
Khatun Baji of Shahr-e Now made my shirt[57]
No housewife made a neater stitch than this bird
My slippers are Shirazi-made *maleki*[58] brand
No other *mashti* has slippers that are that grand
My purse holds one thousand and odd dinar
No other *mashti* has a purse that goes that far."

Another one says: "Oh brothers, in these few days that the worlds lasts, we should have fun. Have not you heard the song of the *mashti*s?

"'What use are cotton drawers with embroidered shawl?
Sell them; a few coins you get to ensnare your doll.
Oh idle *mashti*, drop it and finish it all.
With felt hat, ducklike tresses, be mindful don't fall,
If you were hit and killed, you son of a bitch,
Let it be, go and finish the stitch.'"

In short, in another corner another group had gathered who smoked, gazed, and sighed like the poet Moshtari said:

Last night I went to the *luti*s' hangout
I saw, sitting around, a bunch of louts
Hotly discussing the price of copulation
Among them it created some vexation
One grieves because his beard is growing
The other sings in praise of beauty and drinking
One says, my arse goes for a golden sovereign
The other answers: yours is not worth a farthing
Suddenly during this heated altercation
This message is heard in loud exclamation

May I be your cover, Oh coverer of debauchees,
My sword is bare, where is your sheath?

In short, this group of people and their wives just like them, from dawn to dusk, walk in the streets and the bazaars and [indulge in] frequent orgies, as the poet has said:

A woman who walks the street
Is not a woman, she is a strumpet.

Truly, Mowlavi appropriately has said:

Every particle in this earth and heaven
Seeks its kind like straw and amber.[59]

God Almighty in the holy Koran has said, "The adulterer does not marry any but an adulteress."[60]

Another group of libertines are nobles and aristocrats. They mostly get their hereditary pensions, and they have nothing to do. For instance, most of the idle Qajars, the dissolute immigrants, rich usurers, and the cheating merchant who leaves his assistant in the shop and goes after his debauchery with his mates. Or the brothers and sons of ministers who have lots of money and no work to do and spend their time in taverns, coffeehouses or inns and gather in a surgeon's shop, in the passageways of the caravansaries, and in the shops of merchants, wherever it may be. They discuss politics and social affairs, and they insist on their point of view. All troubles of our time come from these idle people. From dawn until three hours into the evening, they talk vain words, wander about, and spend their time uselessly. If their poor wives die from stomachache or colic of the colon, they do not have a penny to buy a lump of sugar or medicine to cure them. Without

money, without clothes, the women suffer under these faithless men until God almighty may give them salvation. If I
want to describe some of the faults, words, and stories of this
group, neither my tongue nor my pen will suffice, and my
description will amount to countless pages. These guys are
also found among men, may God's curse be upon them.

> See this inhuman lout
> Who will never see bliss.
> For himself, the easy way out
> For wife and child unhappiness.

Description of Men's Treatment of Women

That which is seen and heard: at the time when a man takes a
woman, a bag full of lies is sent to the wife before he marries
her so that when the wife comes to her husband's house she
has no alternative but to look after her husband. One of the
first requirements of getting married is that he should pay the
bride's money; the men of our time do not pay this. As you
have often heard and seen, they say, "Who has paid it, and
who has received it?" So right from the beginning they do not
intend to pay it. Therefore, a man who does not have one hundred *tuman*s of capital puts up a bride's money payment of five
hundred *tuman*s, and this is the ultimate in cheating and lack
of consideration. God Almighty has said, "Give women their
dues,"[61] and if men would do so, then there wouldn't be any
fighting between man and wife. It is better for them to reduce
the amount but pay it.

With regard to keeping women, God has said: "And treat
them well,"[62] but men do not do even one thousandth of what
God has told them to do with women. There is a famous

12. That Old Libertine! From *Molla Naser al-Din* 8, no. 23 (12 Oct. 1913).

saying that "there is no unfortunate woman who was fortunate for the first forty days of her marriage, but when the time of being fortunate comes to an end, the time of misfortune arrives, and all her good characteristics turn to vices." There is a story that a man was in love with a woman for five years and he suffered greatly; he eventually married her, and after forty days of happiness he one day reluctantly looked at the wife and said: "My dear, there is a spot in your eye; I had not noticed it before." The wife smartly realized what he meant and said, "It has appeared since your love has waned."

> Seen through the eyes of Majnun
> You will see only Leyla's beauty and swoon.[63]

Men who want to marry women, who are madly in love and marry them willingly, behave in this way. Woe the woman who is found by this aunt or that go-between. Such a woman will obviously not be liked by the man, nor will she like him. Some men say, "Until I see whether I like the woman, I will not marry her," and they repeat this famous poem by Sheikh Sa'di that says:

> Oh master, every spring get a new wife
> That old calendar needs a new life.[64]

But it is not like that. You wise men who find fault with women, just imagine, is this the right way to keep a woman and at the end of the year to divorce her? She won't remain without a husband; surely, she will remarry. And that man will keep her for one year and get another wife, so there is no need for marriage. Like animals or like the ways of some religions, you give your wife to your friend and then get his wife. As they say, "In every novelty, there is pleasure." It is good for you; you can do it until you die. Now, really, Sheikh Sa'di, may God bless him, who was one of the great wise man and a great theologian, out of fairness and justice advises them in this way: "What would be the treatment of women by illiterate and common men? What misery they make them suffer."

As they say, there is nothing worse than killing; if a man kills a woman, they do not kill that man.[65] In this way, the blood of a woman is wasted. Poor women—neither can they stand against men nor can they escape them, as if they are saying:

> If you can overpower us
> To God you cannot do thus
> Though strong, not every arm
> Ought to cause the weak harm
> The feelings of the weak do not abuse
> Lest one day you be in their shoes.[66]

Because women are naive and without hatred, however, they suffer at the hands of their husbands; whenever he displays kindness [to them], like children they forget everything.

> Like a child who fights with his mother
> He runs again to her without bother.[67]

This Tradition proves my point, that the Prophet, peace be upon him, has said: "If you tell your wife once, 'I love you,' she will not forget it until she dies, even if you have lied." There is a story that a Turkish man had two wives and two blue beads; he gave one to one wife and the second to the other. When both were present, he would say in Turkish, "The one who has the blue bead, my soul is with her." And those simpletons of women would be very happy and grateful to the husband. But everything requires justice. As God has said in the Koran, "Men can marry four wives, provided that they treat them justly." If you cannot be just, one is better for you. The verse of the Koran is, "If you are not fair, one is for you."[68] In our times, a man who is just is a rarity. If some of the men want to be just, they behave like that Turkish man, and that is cheating, not justice. Because the Koran states, "Mighty is your deception,"[69] men attribute all deceit to women. Through proof and experience, it becomes clear that female deceit comes from men as well. If women know any deceit, they have learned it from men.

> My dear, don't you remember this saying
> That man is the thief of another's nature?[70]

If you want to see the extent of the deceit of men, when they marry two women, they always lie. When they are with the new wife, they say, "The first wife is your slave girl. I wish to God that she would ask for a divorce or die, so you and I would be rid of her." When they are with the old wife, [they say], "My lady, I am your servant and have brought her to serve you. You are the mistress of me and her." May God forgive you this double-talk of yours.

They have truly said that the face of a man with two wives is black, let alone a man with three or four, who has neither this world nor the other. "Truly, he is an absolute failure in this world and the one to come."[71] This is but one of the points of the deceit of men, and God Almighty has said in the Koran, "Indeed, their schemes were sufficient to erase mountains."[72] But this is the way of the faithful and believing man; we take refuge from the monkeylike, inhuman men who do not acknowledge God; what misery they do cause women.

As we have heard and seen at night when the men come home, the poor wife has prepared dinner, beautified herself, and prepared snacks and wine. The wretch of a husband, lower than a son of a gun, enters the house, finds fault with every possible thing, and says, "Why did not you crush shit in the mortar, or why did not you trim my moustache?" He will go to a great extent to find such faults. If somebody does not love his wife, he becomes more ill tempered every moment and wants to pick a fight. "Why did your mother come to our house?" Or "Why did your father say such and such? Dinner was not well done. Why was the table cloth not properly laid?" Or "Why isn't the lamp clean?" Or "The dishes are dirty." Or he goes to another extent and says, "Why have you have applied so much powder on your face? You look like a miller." Or "Why do you have so much rouge on your cheeks? They look as if they are smeared with the blood of an ass." The poor woman, who has made up herself with so much passion and love, hears this [and] despairs of the husband's love. If the woman is very patient, she will not say anything and will end the night in this way, but if the wife is ill tempered and short-sighted and answers even with one word, even if it is only a slight complaint, she will immediately be beaten up, and her bones will be broken. In short, a night as long as the day of resurrection passes for that poor woman, and she does not sleep until morning, and in the morning he gets up and goes out of the house.

Of course, that woman does not have the inclination to talk to the husband and say: "We don't have any money" or "Such and such thing is finished" or "The children are hungry, and they do not have any clothes." When that night was so terrible for that poor woman, what can I say about her day? Being in a miserable condition, beaten up, hungry, with these ungrateful brats, she has to spend out of her own pocket, and if she does not have money, she will have to borrow until the angry husband, who has left the house, comes back. They say, "Noble women, they have to be patient," but until when? Are women not God's creatures? Whatever God settled on them men deny to them. They do exactly the opposite of the divine words. Has not God said in the Koran, "Treat them well or let them go in kindness"?[73] God does not want that any harm and difficulty befall his servants and says, "No one shall be burdened beyond his ability."[74]

Men expect more than women can give. If, for instance, a woman has some property, some inheritance, or some pension or has earned some money by herself, the men use it all and are not at all thankful. It so happened one day that I saw one of my relatives who was telling his wife that whatever the wife has belongs to the husband. I told him: "Are you Jewish?" He said, "No, our religion is like that." I said, "That what you say is Judaism because if a Jewish woman marries and has one hundred thousand *tuman*s, whatever she has becomes the property of the husband and that woman has no right to her own bride's money. But Islam has said in the Koran, 'And for women their share is from what they earn.'"[75] This is God's compassionate decree. That is for their old age and need. As long as a woman is young, everybody is after her and wants to keep her, but in her old age nobody wants her. Children, husband, and all relatives abandon her. The husband marries another woman; the son spends whatever he has on his wife and children; the daughter is busy with her husband and taking care of her children. That poor woman cannot rely on them for comfort. If she has some property in her old age, it will not be bad for her, but if she does not have anything, she will end up in poverty and misery, as they have said:

> Lest you tarry in this world long
> Old age and poverty will wear you down.[76]

In truth, death in such a time is a comfort and a release—especially in our time, when women, because of the tyranny of their husbands, become old so soon. The cruelties of men are very different; some engage in debauchery and sexual improprieties, and some are so cruel and daring that if the woman, even unintentionally, says something senseless, they beat her in such a way that she may die. Some others find fault with whatever women do. Some others behave very haughtily and proudly; they never smile at their wives, and they do not joke or play with them. They make love like a donkey when they mount their wives, or when they engage in sex, it is with beatings and violence. But this is not the proper way. Has not God said in the Koran: "You shall treat them nicely,"[77] not cruelly and roughly? God Almighty has created men and women as lovers for each other, not as oppressor and oppressed.

He whose words enraptured the world used to say,
Talk to me, my little red-haired fay.[78]

If the Prophet of God (peace be upon him) behaved toward his wife in such a manner, why do other men behave in such an [abominable] manner? God be praised that the king of time acts according to the words of the Prophet; as they have said, "People follow their kings."[79] Mowlavi has said:

That true prophet, the guide to what you have to heed,
Has said: "People follow their king's creed."[80]

This has been proven by traditions of civilization, philosophy, and religion and has been experienced, and it is correct because the king is the heart of the world and the turning point of mankind. He is the teacher of the time and the designer of every plan; therefore, the subjects have to abide by the authority of the government; otherwise, they would be leaderless, and then the rules of civilization would come apart, and the glass of life broken. Nobody would be able to possess or undertake anything. Society would be shattered, and its high ideals diminished. Therefore and out of necessity, one has to follow the rules of the kings so that one makes progress every day and gradually one may reach that royal threshold. In this blessed time that Iran is a paradise of the world, the king of kings of Iran, wise and generous Naser al-Din Shah, who is the best of the kings, may God keep his kingdom, behaves like a father in word and deed, and he sets an example to the world. He marries wives from every class, so that they [the class] should not feel neglected. Although as the saying goes, "The kingdom is barren, and the king is not in need of children and wives," we people are his slaves and slave girls and not capable of being his wives. But he out of his absolute compassion behaves with his lowest subject in such a way that she in no time becomes elevated to the heavens. All the relatives of that woman become rich and respectable. It is quite obvious, like the sun in the sky, that the king, who is the prayer direction of the world, behaves in such a way with his handmaidens and talks in such respectful manner with them, so why do other men behave in such an abominable manner? What happened to the saying that "men are followers of their kings"? If the king behaves so wonderfully with so many women, and if the men of Iran would take him as their model, Iran would be a paradise. Then the wife would not complain about her husband, and there wouldn't be any need for quarrel and complaints and not even writing a book, and there wouldn't be even a need to answer *The Education of Women* or to write *The Vice of Men*.

> Loyalty abrogated, gone is chivalry
> Nothing remains of them but names like Simorgh and
>   Alchemy.[81]

An Episode of My Life

The story of this humble author that I promised in the beginning of the book is the following. In the days of youth and the time of happiness, one of the immigrants from Qarabagh[82] fell passionately in love with this Astarabadi girl.

> Since in this heart he sought love of a friend
> Know that in that heart love will be sustained.

Therefore, also, as the saying goes, "Human love comes spontaneously," I fell madly and passionately in love with him. My Moses, like [the prophet] Moses, set the heart of my Sinai aflame, and his miracle-working hand gladdened my face. It became such that even when I was asleep, I could not forget him, and his image would not leave my mind alone even for one moment.

> Love has and will wrought wonders;
> It has turned many turbans into miters.[83]

Unlike him, my relatives were not happy, except for my dear mother, who out of love for her daughter was willing to consent to this marriage. My maternal uncle, who was the head of our family and one of the greatest scholars of that time, was against it, basing himself on Islamic law and custom. We discussed this for four years, and if I describe the pangs of separation from him, I will have to write many tomes.

> Separation has a heart of stone
> Once it is broken, it is all alone.[84]

Since the story of my passionate love is long, I had better be short. At any rate, my mother was content and with lots of difficulty turned my uncle around. With four prayers and four hundred *tuman*s in credit payable whenever he could, our marriage took place. The separation came to an end. That same evening the nuptials happened. It was the custom of my mother that she would marry off her daughters easily—that is, she would not sell them—so that my other sister was married off in the same manner. For a few years, my mother financially helped her son-in-law. At any rate, we got together and away from others.

> The beloved entered drunk with joy
> Like a bursting flower gay and coy
> When that beautiful face I saw
> Was it him? I wondered out of awe.[85]

In short, nothing but his face and his appearance mattered to me, and he was, like me, passionately in love and did not see or notice anyone except me.

> Wisdom weak as wax, the fire-smoldering road
> Only God knows and the one who walked this road.

At the beginning, whatever incidents and difficulties arose, we did not care until the time of childbirth came, and the lamp of passion and delirium was extinguished, and the period of hardship began. It was the time of pregnancy, of giving birth, of moaning and shouting. In short, this humble author became a weak female like others. I had daughters, sons, every day moaning and complaints, and had no time for myself. Every day and night I was wrestling with despair and picking the fruit of disappointment from the branch of disillusion. This moment I was thinking of the wet nurse and the servant, and the other I was thinking of the cost of daily bread. I do not know what to say; I wonder what to write that would not be contrary to my consciousness.

> Between fire and water, I am left wondering,
> His image I see constantly from afar.
> Half of the night awake like Omran's offspring,
> The other half like the son of Azar.[86]

In short, I suffered from these difficulties for nine years and bore six children, four sons and two daughters. Because I did not have milk myself, I had to give them to a wet nurse, but I could not afford it. At last, out of desperation I thought of having a virgin maiden marry my husband so that I could give her instead of myself into the claws of my husband. Although I considered this idea an impossibility and pure imagination, in fact there was no fleeing from it. This idea crept into my mind: "Suppose I could find a woman for my husband, what would happen? I would be the lady of the house, and the household would belong to me, and she would be one of my servants." I convinced myself, won my husband's heart, and made him ready. But at this time my husband was promoted from captain to colonel, and there was a time of disappointment. As I say in this poem:

> The rose garden of love became full of wolfsbane
> See how this poor body of mine was wrought with pain.

Driven to extremities, I was crying and praying to God when suddenly the door opened and an old woman came in.

She greeted me, and I her, and she said: "A while ago you had asked for a servant. There is a widow who has a daughter like a ripe fruit." I said, "Great, and thank you." I rewarded her, and I asked about the girl's family, and she said that she was from peasant stock and originally from Rasht. Four months ago a lady brought her from her town, but the girl did not get along with the lady and left her service. I asked the reason. She said, "The family are poor and destitute. They are hungry and naked, and they were all the time bothering the girl. In this cold winter, she did not even have an overcoat." I said, "How did she manage for the past few months without proper clothes?" She said: "She was sleeping with the son of the lady." I later asked the girl, "Have you become a temporary wife [*sigheh*] of his?" She said, "No, he had wanted to do so, but I did not agree to it." I asked, "How old is your lady's son?" She said: "Twenty." I asked her how many times she had married. She said, "Twice and I have two children." In short, the Rashti woman stayed and began her service. She did not veil herself from any man, stranger or relative. I asked her name. She said, "Hajiyeh Nisa." Day and night she was wrapped in thoughts and wondering as if she was in fear of treachery. I asked her, "Why are you like this?" She said: "I am afraid of the lady who brought me from Rasht. If she finds out where I am, she will come to take her with me; nobody can cope with her because she is a foul-mouthed shrew." I said, "I will change your name so that she won't hear and learn about you." She agreed, and we changed her name to Banu.

After a while, the lady in question found the house, came in like a sweeping wind, and got hold of that Rashti woman. I and my husband with difficulty managed to separate them, and I said, "Why are you fighting? Let us talk so that we know what the problem is." The lady said: "This is the temporary wife of my son, and I paid a fee of four *tuman*s for bringing her from Rasht." The Rashti woman denied it, and turning with a sour face to her, she said, "I do not know you. I have nothing to do with you. Before I beat you up, go away," and whatever curse she knew, she showered them on the lady in question. I thought to myself that the new lady had her share of curses, and I wondered when my share would come. Her former mistress was left bewildered and astounded and kept repeating: "This is my son's wife." I said, "Prove it and satisfy her and take her with you. Since she is a stranger and does not have anyone, and she has taken refuge here, I cannot kick her out of my house." The former mistress said: "Let her be, and you will see what this shameless woman will do to you and how she is going to repay your kindness. She will treat you worse than she did me." She said this and then left the house.

Banu, being assured [of not having to leave], turned to her work. She was a good worker, intelligent, who did not shirk work, but she was evil. I paid every possible kindness to her and did not begrudge her anything; I would give her clothes, a chador, gold jewelry, and more than three months of wages that I had promised her. I would occasionally indirectly mention that she might become the master's *sigheh*.[87] One day, as usual, I went to the royal harem, where I had a relationship with some of the ladies there whom I visited regularly, leaving my husband alone at home with the servants. Because it was New Year (Nowruz) and the tenth of the blessed month of Ramazan, I stayed there four or five nights. When I returned home, because I had organized an annual mourning session for Imam Hoseyn, I gave some money to the servant to buy necessary provisions so that I would not be embarrassed before my guests. But I did not know the truth of the matter that my friend "had become a snake and my day darker than night," as the saying goes. My dear husband had become enamored of that shrewish bitch and had worked out everything. I was not aware of anything, and he was ready to pick a fight with me on something very trivial. Because both of us were fasting, a big fight ensued. In the fight, he told me, "Take whatever you have and go away; otherwise I will kill you." As I heard this and was afraid for my life, I got up and began to gather my belongings. While I was doing so, Banu came in saying: "While you were in the royal harem, somebody came from Rasht." I wanted to go with him, but the master took my chador, hid it, and said, "You can't go," and he did not let me leave. I really did not understand his intent. I could not imagine that the master had ulterior intentions because he did not want me to leave. Since I was absolutely happy with the master and I was proud of myself, I could not imagine that he would be so impassioned with this smelly, lowly servant. Of course, I did not know that, as they say,

> The Alchemist has died out of grief
> The fool has found treasure in the debris.[88]

In short, with tearful eyes and heavy heart I collected my things, and I recited this poem:

> Not a hundred sheep but rather three hundred thousand
> Would not be worthy of not seeing the face of the
>   beloved.[89]

After having collected my belongings, I saw that one of my dresses was missing. I said, "What has become of it, Banu? The nurse had gone to her house, and there was no one but you in the house. Tell me, what have you done with my dress?" She started swearing and saying that she had not taken it, and my husband said: "She is not a thief." I could not say anything because it was no use. At any rate, I packed my things and stayed until the next day in the house, wondering and confused. Whichever of the relatives came and gave advice, it was of no use. My husband said: "Of course you should go." I gave my things to several porters and went to the house of my maternal uncle. After four days, my husband came to see me. He sat like an emperor and did not even ask after my health, and soon he left. I was really bewildered because in the past few years there had never been a fight between us, and if any spat happened, it did not last more than one hour. I had boasted to everyone that it was obvious that my husband was the best of men because he had never been engaged in untoward behavior. After another five days, he came, and after lots of pondering and pretending to be thoughtful, he condescended to say, "What are we to do?" I said: "I am your wife, and I have not come without your consent, and now whatever you say I will do." Then he got up and left. My heart started beating. Why did he behave that way, and why did he leave? Then again I thought that human beings keep on changing their minds. After a few days, he came again, greeted me, and sat down. This time I thought that he had come to make peace, but while we were talking, he became angry. How wonderful was his anger. Again he said, "What are we to do?" I said, "Whatever you decide, I will abide by it." He said, "Do you want a divorce?" I said, "No." He said, "I do not want a seventy-year-old woman who is like my mother." He knew full well that thirty-six years of my unfortunate life had passed and that I was four years older than he was. However roughly he was talking, I answered softly because it was not my own house, and I was tired of these discussions, and I was afraid that he might divorce me. I could not live without him and my children. Already a long time ago I had given away my bride money to him. Therefore, divorcing me would be very easy. And he knew full well that as long as life was within me, God willing, I would not let him go. Again, he started talking harshly with an angry face and said, "I want a wife who does not own even a shirt and comes to me and says, 'I want a shirt.'" Since I had never asked him for anything, not one penny, not one dress, I was astonished and said, "Indeed, if I were a woman who had made frivolous demands on you and made you indebted, you would not talk like this now. I know why you are talking like this. You've got Banu, and now you are fed up with me." He said, "Yes, it is true." He said this with anger and left. I told my relatives after he left,

> Immediately to me it was lucid,
> Like wax in the hand of Rabbi David.[90]

Of course, without any doubt he had made a temporary marriage with Banu and did not know what to do and therefore came with all this faultfinding in me. But after leaving me, my husband was ashamed because he was behaving awfully and trying to cover up his faults. After two more days, he came again; his speech and manners had changed considerably, and he was saying nice things and flattering me. I became friendly, and so we made up. I went back to my house and life. I saw the Rashti woman had become the mistress of the house and in possession of my husband, and my little children were fluttering like frightened chickens under her. Since I was not certain of my husband, I did not say anything, and I behaved extremely accommodatingly. But the Rashti woman was fed up with housework and asked our husband to release her of her marriage contract. My husband did not even ask her to serve out the marriage contract. She stayed a few days so that she had time to take a few things and then she absconded. After quite a bit of investigation, it became obvious that she went to the house of her previous mistress, and whatever she had taken from us she had spent by this time. My husband wanted to send the police after her so that they might arrest and punish her to set an example for all the servants. I was not happy with this, and I forgave her and granted whatever she had taken because apparently she did not have anything.

Anyhow, my husband and I were in love again with each other, as they have said:

Two friends appreciate friendship
When after separation they renew companionship.[91]

One day, while we were talking and joking, I asked him, "How was it that you, my unkind lover, concluded a temporary marriage with Banu? What did I do wrong that you drove me out of the house? I insisted more than you that you should marry her." He said, "While you were in the house, that bitch would not consent to be a temporary wife." He laughed, and I said, "That is a weak excuse." It is similar to the story that I am going to tell:

A man had a slave, and one day the master was going ahead of the slave to the roof. While they were going, the slave "fingered" the master, who turned back and said, "You son of gun, why did you do that?" The slave was very afraid and wanted to give an excuse and said: "Please forgive me, I made a mistake; I thought it was the mistress (Bibi)." This excuse is very appropriate in this context because the name of this humble author also is Bibi.

> I told you a bit of the sorrow of my grieving heart.
> Lest I make you grievous, I stop, for I have too much to
>   impart.

This book has been completed with the help of the Lord.

PART THREE

Women in Persian Satire

Hasan Javadi

From a vixen wife protect us well,
Save us, O God! from the pains of hell.
                    —Sa'di, *Golestan*

Slavery of woman, shah's tyranny and the
        ignorance of populace;
Make a story, which is hard to describe.
                    —Abul Qasem Lahuti

The man-woman relationship has always been one of conflict. Except in early matriarchal societies, man has generally dominated woman, but at the same time he has always been in need of her. Man has enjoyed the advantages of physical strength, political power, wealth, and, until recently, legal status and education, yet his life has never been complete without the presence of woman. This need, threatening both man's sense of pride and his self-sufficiency, has made woman a continuous target of his satire. Doctor Johnson has said, "As the faculty of writing has been chiefly a masculine endowment, the reproach of making the world miserable has always been thrown upon the woman."[1]

Therefore, most satirical works about women express a masculine point of view. A little-known feminist of the seventeenth century, Poulain de la Barre, sums up the whole subject in this way: "All that has been written about women by men should be suspect, for the men are at once judge and party to the lawsuit."[2]

The masculine viewpoint most often expressed is one of aggression toward or victory over women. Sexual jokes, for instance, portray not an act of mutual pleasure, but an act from which only the man benefits. In some languages, the very words for lovemaking have a derogatory connotation.[3] In societies where women are less emancipated, swear words often have sexual associations. This same relationship is true in English, of course, but the number of abusive sexual words in both Persian and Arabic seems to be far greater. One might seek to offend a man by verbally abusing his wife, mother, daughter, or sister. Thus, woman becomes a "sexual object" to be guarded and protected by man. Even references to a man's relationship with his wife or sister are sometimes considered impolite. For instance, even today some men in Iran call their sisters *ham-shireh*, "one who has shared milk with me," or refer to their wives as "the children's mother."

In Persian literature, at least three categories of women are to be found. First, there are women in general; second, saintly women; and third, the beloved. The first category is treated with the most obvious and negative chauvinism, incorporating all the usual prejudices that are common in the East as well as the West. The frame tale of *Thousand and One Nights,* for example, in which Shahrezad prolongs her stories to save herself from impending death, indicates ever-present male suspicion of female infidelity. Similar themes occur in such other Middle Eastern tales as the *Turkish Forty Viziers* and *The Wiles of Women*[4] and the Persian *Tales of a Parrot* and *Bakhtiyar-Nameh.*[5] The works of many Iranian poets also reflect this negative view

of women. The misogynous Jami (816–97/1414–92) arranges
that the hero of his philosophical allegory *Salaman and Absal,*
Salaman, who represents the human soul, is born magically,
not from a woman, so that he is purer than other men. Asadi of
Tus (eleventh century) considers finding a husband a woman's
greatest art, and in one poem he says:

> Outside of women is green and lush as a tree,
> But inside they have venom as the fruit.[6]

Naser Khosrow (d. 395–481/1003–88) brings in yet another
characteristic opinion:

> Since women are imperfect in faith and reason
> Why should men follow their way and decision?[7]

Jami, alluding to the biblical story of creation, asks:

> Woman was fashioned from the left rib;
> Who has ever seen right come from the left?[8]

According to some nationalistic Iranian scholars, women
enjoyed a better status in pre-Islamic Iran, and it was as
a result of the association with the Semitic Arabs that they
became subordinate to men.[9] But such generalizations exalt-
ing the Aryans over the Semites are difficult to justify. The
Aryan Hindus, for instance, practiced the custom of suttee,
burning the Hindu widow on her husband's funeral pyre,
until the nineteenth century. In Zoroastrianism, although a
woman can own property and is urged to learn the sciences
and the arts, there are still many prejudices against her. A religious Pahlavi text says, "Do not be forthcoming with women
so that your toil will not reap repentance and shame. Do not
confide secrets to them so that your toil will not be wasted."[10]

Zoroaster, like Moses and Manu, decreed that if a woman
bears a daughter, the period of purification should be longer
than that for one who gives birth to a boy because the former
has brought to the world a source of sin.[11] The fourth-century
priest Arda Viraf, in an account of heaven and hell that is not
unlike the *Divine Comedy,* describes the terrible punishments
meted out to wives who have disobeyed their husbands.[12]

One of the major sources of information about the condition of women in pre-Islamic Iran is Ferdowsi's great epic *Shah-
Nameh.* Some of his great heroines—Rudabeh, Tahmineh,
Gord-afarid, Katayun, and Ferangis—are worthy companions
to the heroes of this famous work. But other women, such as
Sudabeh and Malekeh, are vicious and treacherous. The former corresponds to Phaedra, and the latter brings death to her
father, an Arab chieftain, as a result of the love she bears for
Shapur, the Sassanid monarch:

> When you hear this story from beginning to end,
> It will suit you better not to follow women.
> Do not seek but pious women in the world;
> Ill-fated women bring shame on you.
> Women and dragons may lie in the dust;
> May the world be purged of these evils.[13]

The advent of Islam changed the status of women. In pre-
Islamic Arabia, where murdering infant daughters by burial was
common, the call of Islam to consider not only rich and poor
but also men and women as equals in the eyes of God and the
statement that "the most virtuous of you is the dearest to God"
were significant revolutions. Although women had become the
spiritual equals of men, they still had a long way to go socially.
Even the Koran, which puts women in charge of men in such

matters as inheritance, testifying, and polygamy, states, "Good women are the obedient, guarding in secret that which Allah hath guarded. As for those from whom ye fear rebellion, admonish them and banish them to beds apart, and scourge them."[14]

The seclusion that was imposed on Moslem women in the centuries to come and that consequently deprived them of many social activities was not propounded by Islam, however. In the early days of Islam, women were in fact freer in their associations with men. For instance, 'Ayesha, the youngest wife of the Prophet, was actively involved in politics after his death and even fought with 'Ali, the Prophet's cousin, on the issue of succession. Zainab, the daughter of 'Ali, who was brought as a captive to the court of the Umayyad caliph Yazid after the tragedy of Kerbela, boldly stood up and gave a fiery speech that made Yazid ashamed. It was only later, as a result of further urbanization of the Arabs and the increasing number of female slaves brought from various parts of the Islamic Empire, that the Umayyads and Abbasids, following the example of the Sassanid kings and other rulers of the time, confined their women to seraglios. As the nomadic simplicity of the old days was replaced with luxury and often corruption, men grew more and more suspicious of and tyrannical toward women.

Tales of women's untrustworthiness found ever-wider currency, and folk sayings concerning women began to circulate. A typical piece of advice was, "Consult them, but do the opposite." Such biased views even contradicted some of the basic teachings of Islam. The Prophet had said, "Learning is a duty for every Moslem man and woman," but later views expressed on the education of women were very different. Qabus Ibn Voshmigir (d. 403/1012), the ruler of Gorgan and Tabaristan, believed that women's learning should not exceed the knowledge of the Koran and the laws of the faith. He said that a woman should not be taught "penmanship."[15] Two moralists and philosophers of later periods, Naser al-Din Tusi (d. 672/1274) and Jalal al-Din Davani (d. 907/1502 or 908/1503), believed that girls should not be taught writing and reading.[16] The latter added, "They should be taught housekeeping and be sent to their husband's house soon."[17] Molla Mohammad Baqer Majlesi (d. 1627/1700), the great Shi'ite theologian, even makes the teaching of the Koran to girls subject to censorship, leaving out the amorous story of Joseph and Potiphar's wife. Then he adds that one should not allow one's daughter to sit in the upper chamber and watch the passersby, but that she should be married off as soon as possible.[18] It was also commonly believed that the stories of such legendary lovers as Leyla and Majnun, Khosrow and Shirin, and Vis and Ramin are inappropriate for women.[19]

But not all women were seen to deserve such distrust, and a limited number were considered "good, pious, and obedient." In his epic *Garshasep Nameh*, Asadi of Tus makes one of the characters thus answer the legendary king Jamshid, who was suspicious of women:

> Delaram said, "O all-knowing and wise king,
> Not every woman will be double-hearted and ten-tongued.
> Not everyone has the same temper and character;
> Even the fingers of two hands are not the same."[20]

Writers sometimes set standards to define a pious wife. Mohammad 'Awfi (ca. 531–633/1176–1236) wrote in his *Javame' ul-Hikayat*, "One should know that when God Almighty's blessings come to someone who is imperfect, she will be more exalted than the men of the world. Though their creation has been from the wrong bone and crookedness imbued in their nature, yet there are many women whose two-foot veil is by far more respected and honored than the thirty-foot turban of men. And no blessing is greater for a man than a pious wife."[21] The writer goes on to give examples of such women. In one story, a woman succeeds in returning to her husband with her virtue unsullied even after many incredible adventures. Unstained virtue was, of course, one of the characteristics of the ideal woman.

The poems written on ideal women somewhat resemble European encomiums, of which the best example is *The Legend of Good Women* by Chaucer. There he shows the expectations that the men of his age had toward their wives. These expectations do not vary greatly between the West and the East. Men wanted their wives to be extremely patient, chaste, and restrained in their conduct and dress. In the lands of Islam, it was always suggested that if a woman tolerated an ugly and ill-tempered husband, she would be amply rewarded in the world to come.[22]

Some of these expectations still persist in the Middle East. For instance, virginity is a precondition of matrimony, whereas a man with no premarital relationships is considered to be "slow" or, at best, "unsophisticated." Awhadi of Maragheh (669–738/1271–1338) sums up in one of his poems the attitude not only of his contemporaries, but of many generations to come:

A veiled wife is a candle for the house;
A coquette is a calamity at all times.
An unchaste wife is an evil lot;

Get rid of her soon as she is a pang to the heart.
A pious spouse fond of obedience and devotion,
Will be like a kernel in one shell with you.
If the wife goes out, beat her hard;
If she wantonly displays herself, strip her naked.
If she does not obey, destroy her;
If she brings shame to you, in the dust bury her.[23]

Then we come to the second category, saintly women, which is one level above the chaste wife, where one finds the mother. The mother in Islamic tradition has a fairly elevated status, and she is regarded in a totally different light than other women. A well-known saying of the Prophet states, "Heaven is under the feet of mothers." Saintly women and great Sufi women also enjoy a venerated status, which reminds one of a similar tradition in Christianity. In the latter religion, Eve and the Virgin Mary are placed in two completely contrasting categories. Sin came into the world through Eve; redemption became possible because of Mary. Although Islam obviously does not subscribe to this mythology, it nonetheless divides women into these two categories: mothers and saints on the one hand and women in general on the other.

Even under very adverse conditions, great and learned women, such as Rabi'a al-'Adawiyya (d. 134/752) and the famous Babi poet and scholar Quratu'l-'ayn (killed in 1268/ 1852), did appear. Rabi'a al-'Adawiyya was among the greatest of saintly women of Islam. Despite the views held by many men of her time that women could not reach heights of sainthood, she gained exactly such stature. Her piety and asceticism, in fact, became proverbial throughout the Islamic world. A tyrannical governor of Basra, who was sent by the notorious

Hajjaj ibn Yusef, was so impressed by Rabi'a that he repented and became an ascetic himself.[24]

Though Rabi'a's position as one of the greatest Sufis was well established, and 'Attar ranked her with the Virgin Mary in his *Biographies of the Saints,* at least one instance of anti-feminism in her time was expressed by a visitor, but he was silenced by her witty answer. He asked her, "All virtues have been bestowed on men, the crown of magnanimity has been placed on men's heads, and the girdle of generosity is for them, and no woman has become a prophet, so then why do you boast so much?" Rabi'a answered, "All that you said is true, but egotism, self-love, selfishness, and [sayings such as] 'I am your Great God'[25] have not come from woman. And a woman has never been a sodomite."[26]

Of the categories of women enumerated earlier, the third one is woman as the "beloved" in Persian literature, which is totally different from either type described previously. It is in fact incredible that the poets with such degrading views of women can be so absolutely humbled by and devoted to the "beloved." These poets consider themselves the "dust of her threshold" and a "captive in her beautiful tresses." Of course, sometimes they are referring to the "Divine Beloved," who is beyond any human perception and imagination; but their sentiments are very often directed toward female beauty as well. Even a Sufi poet such as Jami, with an unmistakably unworldly nature, describes feminine beauties in some of his poems with such gusto and realistic detail and such an amorous passion that one wonders how to explain the misogynous views present in his other poems.

This trend in Persian poetry is reminiscent of the courtly tradition in Europe. Although the poet most likely treated his wife with a lack of civility, he traditionally humbled himself beyond all limits before his imaginary or actual beloved. The Persian poets similarly praised the beloved's beauty and coquetry and even considered her faithlessness, cruelty, and lack of consideration as attractive qualities. But when considering the issue of women in general, their views were very different.

Surveying the antifeminist literature of the West—from the Sixth Satire of Juvenal to the harsh sayings of the Church Fathers (such as Saint Augustine) and their medieval followers[27] and from Chaucer's picture of a shrewd and bossy woman in the *Wife of Bath's Tale* to Molière's witty and graceful satire in *Les précieuses ridicules* and *Les femmes savantes* or Pope's biting remarks in "On the Character of Women"—one finds many similarities to the views held by men of the East. In fact, some of the antifeminist and satirical tales included in the *Discipliria clericalis* of Petrus Alfonsi, the *Decameron,* and the French fabliaux are the same as the tales of the *Arabian Nights,* the *Bakhtiyar-Nameh,* and the *Sindbad-Nameh.*[28] Comparing the antifeminist satirical tradition in Europe and Iran, one finds that for many centuries similar views and often identical stories existed in Europe and in Iran. However, in Iran, the feminist movement did not begin until much later than in Europe, and even then it was inspired by Western influences.

The rule of the Safavids in the sixteenth century, characterized by religious zeal and theocratic administration, was certainly one of the factors in preventing women from gaining their rights. One of the great theologians of a later time, Molla Ahmad Naraghi (d. 1244/1828–29), went to the extreme of forbidding women to participate in religious ceremonies.[29] As westernization gained ground at the turn of the twentieth century, the emancipation of women and the lifting of the veil were among the most often discussed subjects. In modern times, the Iranian poets often complained of the seclusion of women and their lack of participation in social affairs.

As a whole, satirical works concerning women in Iran can be divided into two main periods: one before the impact of the West is felt in the country and the other afterward, when attempts at the emancipation of Iranian women begin. In the first period, a traditional and medieval attitude persists in the literature. Women are often depicted as lustful and not worthy of trust; the harems are full of intriguing women; and the men even prefer boys to women. In the second period, the attitudes change. The chastity of women is essential, but being veiled does not necessarily prevent them from yielding to temptation. Women's superstition and ignorance are often ridiculed, and they are urged to look up to their European sisters for inspiration. When in due course they gradually become too westernized in the eyes of Iranian men, their wastefulness, artificiality, and affected mannerisms become the topics of satire.

Descriptions of women's infidelity and lustfulness abound in classical Persian literature. In a risqué story, Rumi describes how a maidservant contrives, by means of a hollowed-out gourd, to lie with an ass. The gourd is used to prevent penetration and possible injury of her by the ass. The servant's mistress, however, who discovers her "in the act," fails to perceive the gourd. On a pretext, she sends the maid on an errand and tries to satisfy her own insatiable lust. The maidservant returns to find her mistress dead, a victim of her own ignorance and lust. Rumi gives the story an allegorical interpretation, saying that lust makes "an ass seem like a Joseph, and fire like light."[30]

Although in most of his stories Rumi is usually after elucidation of mystical or moral points, some of his stories are the same antifeminist tales that are found in the medieval Eastern or Western sources. Here is another story from the *Mathnavi* with a similar sentiment. A *dalqak* (jester) explains to a great man of religion why he has married a prostitute:

> One night a Seyyed Ajjal said to Dalqak, "You have
>   married a harlot in haste.
> You might have disclosed this [matter] to me, so that we
>   might have made a chaste [woman] your wife."
> Dalqak replied, "I have [already] married nine chaste and
>   virtuous women: they became harlots, and I wasted
>   away with grief.
> I married this harlot without [previous] acquaintance
> in order to see how this one [also] would turn out in the
>   end.
> Often I have tried [sound] intelligence; henceforth,
>   I will seek a nursery for insanity."[31]

On the subject of salacious women, many more examples can be given. Pindar of Rey, an eleventh-century poet known for his poems in the local dialect, wittily describes an old woman who becomes alarmed by a sermon when she remembers her past amorous adventures:

> On a pulpit in Rey once a preacher most vain
> Did deliver a sermon in somewhat this vein:
> Seven members of your body on Judgment Day,
> Will give testimony to what they did, aye![32]
> An old woman did beat at her privates and say,
> What a braggart you'll turn out to be on that day![33]

Shrewish wives and quarrelsome in-laws also become the subjects of satire. Among the scenes of marital life described by Persian classical poets, two instances deserve inclusion here. The first is a well-known episode in the long and adventurous life of Sa'di (610–91 or 615–91/1213–92 or 1219–92), as we know it from his own fictionalized account; the second is a humorous letter written by Qa'ani (1233–70/1808–54) to his royal patron, Naser al-Din Shah. Sa'di's story relates his captivity at the hands of the Crusaders and his ransom by a Syrian friend:

> I had grown weary of the Society of my Damascus friends, and therefore made my way into the Jerusalem desert, where I enjoyed the companionship of the beasts; until the time came when the Franks made me their prisoner, and kept me with Jews in a trench at Tripoli digging clay. One of the leading citizens of Aleppo, with whom I had been formerly acquainted, chancing to pass by recognized me, and said, "Sirrah, what manner of life is this?" I said, "What can I say:
>
>> I fled from men to mountain and to plain,
>> For I had nothing from mankind to gain;
>> How is my case? Regard me in this den,
>> Where I must sweat with men that are not men."
>> Better to hang in chains, when friends are there,
>> Than dwell with strangers in a garden fair.

> He had compassion on my condition, and with ten dinars procured my release from bondage. He took me along with him to Aleppo, and there made me marry his daughter, adding a dowry of a hundred dinars. Some time passed. She was a woman always scowling—disobedient and growling; she began to give me plenty of her shrewish tongue, and made life wholly miserable for me.

> A bad wife comes with a good man to dwell,
> She soon converts his present world to hell;
> Beware of evil partnership, beware—
> From hellish torment, Lord, thy servants spare!

Once in a torrent of abuse she said, "Are you not that man whom my father bought back from the Franks?" I said, "Yes, I am that man whom he bought back from the Frankish chains for ten dinars, and delivered into your bondage for a hundred dinars."[34]

Qa'ani, in a letter that is written in an ingeniously rhythmic prose, describes how the fighting between his two mothers-in-law ends in a fire that leaves him homeless. At the end, in the tradition of panegyric poets, he makes an appeal to the generosity of his royal patron. Here I give a partial translation of this letter but ask for the reader's understanding that the translation does not do justice to the beauty and satirical tone of the original:

Now for many years I have been afflicted with two unruly spouses, who are quick in anger and slow in discretion. One calls herself the "Honored Beloved" and the other the "Beautiful Blossom." One has secured a genealogy, tracing herself back to the tribe of Qavanlu, and the other has procured a scroll, establishing her ancestry in the family of Davanlu.[35] Though I have always tried to keep them both happy, every day they start a brawl and every night a quarrel.

I have two shrewish and intriguing mothers-in-law, who are ugly of face, unpleasant in shape, greedy in taste, fearless, and unclean. They are as old as the world itself and more wicked and bloodthirsty than Hind, the Eater of Livers.[36] It is as if Ferdowsi had them in mind when he said:

> 'Tis better both woman and dragon be buried in the
> dust
> So that the world free from them both may rest.

They are so full of spite and malice that [Your Majesty's] servant cannot describe but one of their thousand schemes. For instance, the other day, under a womanish pretext, they scattered dust in the arena of wrestling and like two novice champions were engaged in the sport. Before long, their faces were black from slapping and blue from shoe-inflicted blows. They left each other pale, bloodstained, wounded, and in great confusion, with their hair pulled and their dresses torn.

The Qavanlu mother, finding herself beaten and defeated, ran to the house of her relatives and chided them for their indifference. Seeing such a hue and cry, they rushed out in her defense armed with sticks and clubs. While clamoring in the Turkish manner and applauding like Arab women, the maidservants with ladles and skimmers scurried to the house. There was absolute chaos, and the neighbors came out to watch.[37]

Qa'ani goes on to describe how the Qavanlu wife and her mother threw out their rival's duenna and set fire to her *korsi,* a heating device shared by the duenna and the other mother-in-law, and as a result burned the whole house down.

It was because of such family feuds that 'Obeyd-e Zakani, one of the greatest satirists of Iran, writes, "Don't seek comfort, peace, and happiness in the house of a man who has two wives."[38] In his "Definitions," a succinct and humorous description of the people of his age, 'Obeyd-e Zakani devotes the ninth and tenth sections to "the householder and what pertains to him" and "the true nature of men and women," respectively. Both sections are very revealing:

The Bachelor: He who laughs at the world's beard.

The Unfortunate: The householder.

The Two-Horned [Dhu'l-Qarnayn]: He who has two wives.

The Most Unfortunate of the Unfortunate: He who has more.

The Sour-faced Cuckold: the father-in-law.

The Futile: The householder's life.

The Wasted: His time.

The Dissipated: His wealth.

The Distracted: His mind.

The Bitter: His life.

The Abode of Mourning: His house.

. . .

The Kinsman: His deadly foe.

Joy after sorrow: The triple divorce.

. . .

The Lady: She who has many lovers.

The Housewife: She who has few.

The Virtuous: She who is satisfied with one lover.

The Maiden: A name denoting what does not exist.[39]

Prearranged marriages and injunctions against seeing one's wife until the nuptials are among other subjects of satire. 'Obeyd-e Zakani relates in his *Resaleh-ye Delgosha* several such stories. Majd al-Din Hamgar, a contemporary poet from

Yazd, who apparently finds himself stuck with an old wife after the marriage, is the subject of several stories in this collection of anecdotes. When the poet went from Yazd to Isfahan, he left his wife behind, but she soon followed him. The news of her arrival was brought to the poet by his servant, who said, "Good news! Your lady has alighted at the house." "Good news," replied Majd al-Din, "would rather be that the house alighted on her!" The lady, to whom this speech was reported, reproached her husband for his unkind words, saying that "the world has existed long before you and me and no one has treated a lady in this manner." She quotes a poem by Omar Khayyam that begins: "Days changed to nights, ere you were born or I."⁴⁰ "Before me, perhaps," replied Majd al-Din, "but Heaven forbid that day and night should have existed before you!"⁴¹ In another story, a man marries a woman through the importunity of his friends and, as was customary with the Moslems, saw the bride's face for the first time on the marriage night. She proves to be very ugly or, at best, perhaps merely "plain looking." A few days after the nuptials, she says to him, "My life! As you have many relatives, I wish you would inform me before which of them I may unveil." "My soul!" responds the husband, "if you will but conceal your face from me, I care not to whom you show it."⁴²

Some poets advise men not to marry. 'Obeyd-e Zakani says, "Do not marry if you don't want to become a cuckold!"⁴³ Sana'i (d. 535/1141), whose misogynous views are strongly voiced throughout his *Divan*, believes that a young slave boy can be a man's partner at night as well as a traveling companion at daytime. He says, "The Egyptian Joseph suffered ten years of prison because of a woman. If this happened to a 'friend of God,' what will happen to you?"[44] Then the poet recommends that one should be like a cock that does not confine himself to a single hen. Sana'i compares having a slave girl, who is one's own property, with a wife, who is a creditor. The explanation is that in Islam the wife can have her marriage portion whenever she wishes to, and because it is often paid when there is a divorce, the husband is always in debt to her:

> Don't marry! Leave aside women in this springtime:
> No man marries if he is in his right mind.
> . . .
> If you are a slave of passion, buy a bondsmaid,
> Beautiful, fair-faced, comely, and well shaped.
> As long as you wish, she will comply with your desires.
> When you don't want her, she will be ready cash.
> It is much better to rise in the morning
> To see the face of your own property than that of a
>   creditor.[45]

The views quoted so far picture a society that is plagued with immorality, hypocrisy, and distrust of women. This was particularly the case in the Mongol period and especially among the ruling class of Iran. 'Obeyd-e Zakani gives in his *The Ethics of the Aristocrats* a vivid picture of this age that reminds the reader of the satires of Juvenal at the time of Rome's decadence. In the chapter "On Chastity," Zakani writes about the great men of his age, who considered chastity something of the past and believed that "the ancients have made a great mistake on the subject and have wasted their precious lives in ignorance and error." The aristocrats of Zakani's time believed that "it is impossible to enjoy life without playing and indulging in vices and forbidden pleasures."[46] 'Abbas Eqbal, a modern Iranian historian, writes about the later part of the Mongol period (fourteenth century): "The mother of one of the kings was known for prostitution and promiscuity; the wife of another kills her husband in the most hideous way because he had imprisoned her lover; another king blinds his father with his own hands and commits adultery with his mother; and a fourth monarch forces his enemies to divorce their wives so that he may woo them and write *ghazals* of his love for them."[47]

Three centuries later we discover still another picture of moral decadence when Iran was in turmoil and the Afghan invasion imminent. The country was ruled at this time by Shah Sultan Husain (1105–35/1694–1722), who was so incapable of running the affairs of state that he left everything to the discretion of his court ministers, eunuchs, and mollas. Even when the Afghan invasion had laid siege to Isfahan, he was not aware of the real situation. An interesting satirical work entitled *Rostam al-Tavarikh,* written by Mohammad Hashem Asef in 1247/1832, contains numerous passages on the amorous life of Shah Sultan Husain and at the same time depicts the prevailing moral decadence at the court of Isfahan. There is an ironic duality in the life of the monarch as pictured in this book. He is very religious and something of a theologian and scholar, yet he has no scruples about marrying other men's wives. Though the writer, Mohammad Asef, directs his criticism mostly toward the mollas and ministers at the court of Isfahan, he also gives a vivid picture of the condition of women in the royal harem. He writes of Sultan Husain:

> Day and night he was eager and without restraint in eating and coition. As a test in one day and night, he ordered one hundred virgins to be taken into temporary wedlock,

in accordance with the Shari'a and with their own and their fathers' consent, and in twenty-four hours as a result of a great aphrodisiac that Refuge of the Nation and the Land deflowered all those lovely girls and graceful and sugar-lipped sweethearts and still like an intoxicated bachelor was eager for more. Then in compliance with the law of the Prophet, he divorced and sent them back to their homes with legal marriage portions and with precious clothes and ornaments presented by the Monarch of the World. As this story spread throughout the land of Iran, whoever had a wife uniquely beautiful would willingly and eagerly divorce her and send her to the royal court, which is renowned for justice, out of expediency or in the hope of an ample reward. The Matchless Monarch of the World, in accordance with religious rites, would marry and enjoy her, and then he would similarly divorce and dismiss her. The lady, being thus graced with royal favors, would return to her husband with bounty and riches.[48]

The second phase of the satirical treatment of women begins in the nineteenth century, and it is in sharp contrast with the earlier phase. Here the satirist tries to condemn and criticize the backwardness, ignorance, and superstitions of Iranian women, hoping that by doing so he will press them toward progress and self-reform. The achievements and advancements of the Western woman are very often in the satirist's mind, and sometimes she is offered as a model for her Iranian counterpart. This attitude persists until, as a result of the steady westernization of Iranian women, a new attitude emerges. The criticism of the satirist is then directed toward too much artificiality and senseless imitation of Western women.

One of the earliest satirical works that constructively criticizes the manners and superstitions of Iranian women is the
famous book *Kulsum Naneh,* or *The Beliefs of Women,*[49] which
has been attributed to Agha Jamal Khunsari.[50] A famous theologian and judge of the Safavid period, Agha Jamal was, unlike
many ulema of his time, a generous, liberal, and extremely
witty man. *The Beliefs of Women* is written in the form of a
theological treatise such as those often composed by highly
respected ayatollahs in order to advise their followers on various religious and social problems. In this satirical little book,
three experienced and roguish old ladies discuss with Kulsum
Naneh various questions pertaining to a woman's life and give
the most authoritative and "beneficial" pieces of advice. In a
recent edition of the book, the editor notes, "One important
point to remember is that in *The Beliefs of Women* the writer's intention was not to collect folklore but to ridicule the
beliefs and superstitions of the women of his time and more
particularly the women of Isfahan. Furthermore, considering the social milieu of the author, one might say that this
ridiculing is also directed to that group of people who had
accepted a multitude of unfounded quotations as indisputable
principles and obvious facts, or at least they outwardly con-
ceded to them, considering themselves amongst the *ulema;* as
if the writer of the book had wanted to say that [such men and
women] are of the same leaven."[51] Kulsum Naneh acknowl-
edges that although many women keenly observed religious
ablutions, they would forget about them if it meant spoil-
ing their makeup. The writer says: "When you have painted
your nails and created patterns on your hands with henna,
or painted your eyebrows, it is necessary to forsake partial or
complete ablutions [*vozu* and *ghusl*]. If a woman has a slave

girl at home and she thinks that by going to the public bath she will give her husband the chance to sleep with the girl, she should forsake the complete ablution until the obstacle is removed."[52] Kulsum Naneh has said that this could be for a week, and some people believe that it could be for more. The writer humorously notes the discrepancy in the veiling habits that Iranian women observe:

> The men from whom one should be veiled include every turbaned man, even though he is less than fifteen years old. The bigger the turban, the more its wearer should be avoided, particularly students of theology in whatever dress they might be. . . . But the opposite group from whom one should not be veiled includes Jewish peddlers, grocers, cloth merchants, physicians, fortune-tellers, exorcists, minstrels, etc. . . . If the Jewish peddler happens to be a fortune-teller as well, you should associate with him as much as possible. Avoiding him is considered a cardinal sin. If he enters your house, you should respect him and fulfill his desires.[53]

Chapter 9 of *The Beliefs of Women,* devoted to the relationship between husband and wife, features the experienced ladies teaching the young women how to dominate their husbands:

> The female scholars are unanimous that the bride should behave as an enemy toward her mother-in-law and sister-in-law, and they should reciprocate. Though they might be friends at heart, outward animosity is a must. But Bibi Shah Zeinab, quoting her great master, the accursed Iblis, has said, "The bride should do exactly the opposite of whatever the mother-in-law says, and the latter should always

complain of her daughter-in-law to her son. Similarly, the wife should calumniate her sister-in-law as much as possible. Also it is an obligation for the wife to quote numerous accusations and lies from the accursed Satan to her husband, and whenever the mother- in-law follows and tries to beat her, she should scratch her." Kulsum Naneh has said, "Whenever there is a fight between them, they should fiercely bite each other's privates. . . . The wife who is hurt must capitalize on this when she sleeps with her husband, putting the blame on the sister-in-law, so that he will be less friendly with her, and perhaps she will frequent their house less often.[54]

Although *The Beliefs of Women* criticizes the ridiculous beliefs and customs of Iranian women, the author's intention is not to emancipate them to the level of European women, but rather to bring them into conformity with Islamic ideals as preached by the clerics of that period. The book has many positive points, but the Safavid period was not ready for Western ideas of female emancipation. It was not until the turn of the twentieth century that the role of women in society began to change. Even after the Constitutional Revolution in 1906, the fanatical views that kept women in seclusion were only grudgingly modified. The conservatives who opposed the Constitution claimed that its passage "will permit drunkenness, tolerate vices, allow women to go unveiled and abrogate the Shari'a."[55] When the full-scale education of women became a topic of controversy, some men considered it outrageous—similar to "allowing alcoholic drinks or spreading prostitution."[56] Even some of the liberal constitutionalists could not bring themselves to allow women to go unveiled or to take part in social activities. These things were considered anti-Islamic. Keeping this in mind, the reader should realize what stiff opposition was met when such writers and poets as 'Ali Akbar Saber, Yahya Dowlatabadi, Lahuti, 'Ali Akbar Dehkhoda, 'Eshqi, Jalal al-Mamalek Iraj Mirza, and many others raised the issue of emancipation of women.

One of the early progressive poets who defended the rights of women was Jelveh of Ardestan (d. 1313/1896). He, curiously enough, was a lifelong bachelor who led a life of celibacy. In the following poem, he humorously takes up the subject of polygamy:

> One night a girl sweet and fair shaped,
> Asking a question of her mother said:
> "O Mother, I have a problem
> From which my heart is in flame.
> Why has our wise Prophet allowed
> A man several wives to wed
> But that most sage and learned one
> Of men for women did not grant but one?"
> A deep sigh heaved the mother,
> Which made the daughter even sadder,
> And said, "Since the Prophet was a man,
> So he allowed several wives for a man.
> For sure, if the Prophet had been a woman
> Several husbands would be part of the plan.
> O my darling, good women suffer most
> As from womenfolk has never a prophet come forth."[57]

The Azerbaijani poet and satirist 'Ali Akbar Saber (1278–1329/1862–1911) at the turn of the twentieth century made the issue of women one of the main topics of his subtle and skillful satire. Although he wrote his poems in Turkish, he had great impact on the satirical literature of Iran in the constitutional period. Not only were most of his poems that were published mainly in the famous journal *Molla Naser al-Din* immediately translated into Persian by Sayyed Ashraf of Gilan, but his poems were also widely popular in the Turkish-speaking regions of Iran.

Superstitious, ignorant women and chauvinistic men are Saber's subjects. On the whole, however, he holds men responsible for the degraded state in which women find themselves. The characters he depicts are typical and true to life. In a poem entitled "Don't Let Him Come," a fifteen-year-old girl is hoodwinked into marrying a man as old as her father in the belief that he is much younger. When she finds out that he is an old man, she exclaims her loathing for his white hair, his chimney-like hat, his body odor, and, in short, the very sight of him:

O Auntie, don't let him come!
His sight is hateful, don't let him come!
O God, it's as if he is not human,
His face is not like any other man.
For love of God, he is no husband for a woman.
He is a devil and a swine, don't let him come!
The sight of him is hateful, don't let him come!

I was too shy to inquire when betrothed;
"He is young and nice," I was told.
This could be my husband! Heavens, what a thought!
O Auntie, don't let him come!
His doings are hateful, don't let him come!

A chimneylike hat he prefers to wear,
His eyebrows are bespecked with white hair.
Though he seems as old as my father fair,
He is a swindler, don't let him come!
His doings are hateful, don't let him come![58]

The men of Saber's poems proudly talk of divorcing their wives and getting new ones. In "The March of the Old Men,"[59] we find "an old man who lives like a ram." Having four wives, every year he marries and divorces three or four more. He is outwardly pious. He wears a beard, puts on an agate ring as a sign of religiosity, and never forgets his prayers or fasting, yet he is a dirty old man who not only pursues young women but makes passes at handsome boys. In another poem, a man from Ardabil has gone to Baku, where he sees so many beautiful "madames" on the streets and boulevards, in the theaters, and at circuses that he grows bewildered. Becoming convinced that it has been an absolute waste to live in his small and provincial hometown, where he has not been able to see one female face unveiled on the streets, he vows, "I will never mention your name, O Ardabil!"

Women become the subjects of Saber's satire as well. In a poem entitled "Advice of an Old Witch,"[60] young brides are instructed in how to make the best of their lives. Because no faithful husband can possibly be found, a woman should spend her husband's earnings on her women friends and be happy with them behind his back. The poem "Complain"[61] satirizes prearranged marriages. The illiterate wife of a poet describes her sad life after marrying an intellectual who lives completely in his own world. The wife, coming from a family where not a single book could be found, regards her husband as insane for poring over books and scribbling poetry. Saber gives a hilarious picture of the misunderstanding between a husband and wife whose values are at variance.

Even 'Ali Akbar Dehkhoda (1258–1338 Sh/1879–1959), best known for his authoritative dictionary, entered this dialogue in his early and famous satirical essays (1324–26/1907–1909) referred to as *Charand Parand*. In one essay, Dehkhoda relates the story of a one-time camel driver, Hajji Molla 'Abbas, who, after spending all his money to get concubines in Qom, is initiated by a sympathetic molla into the circle of clergy. Thereafter, Molla 'Abbas prospers. Marrying the orphaned daughter of a merchant, he uses her money in the pursuit of his pleasure while giving her no chance of happiness in return. His profession affording him many privileges, his life is occupied solely with exchanging one concubine for another.[62] In another essay, Dehkhoda answers the letter of an imaginary reader of *Sur-e Esrafil* whose name is "Asir-e Joval Khanum" (Lady Captive in a Sack)! She has complained that her children die in infancy, and Dehkhoda gives her a ridiculous prescription that is a combination of witchcraft and old, popular herbal medicine. Dehkhoda even at this early stage of his career shows an amazing familiarity with the idioms as well as the superstitions of Tehrani women.

A poet who followed Saber and wrote exclusively in Azerbaijani was Mo'jez of Shabistar (1253–1313 Sh/1874–1934), who made the victimization of women the foremost problem in Iranian society. He considered the women of rural areas much more deprived of their rights than their sisters in Tehran or Tabriz. They are poorer, more superstitious, and less educated and therefore more prone to suffer from male chauvinism and demagogical clerics. Mo'jez refers to sexual relations as an act that is not consensual as far as women are concerned because it is often forced upon them as a duty owing to their ignorance and poverty. In numerous satirical poems, Mo'jez depicts the plight of women, forced marriages of underage girls with older men, and the laws governing marriage that give the right of divorce to the man. In a poem entitled "When Will They Know?" he writes,

> O God, when will these people show
> their inclination toward high-heeled shoes?
> O fortune-teller! Look into your bowl, and let us know
> when the sisters will become newspaper readers.
> How long will the demon of ignorance and despotism
> be the guide of the womenfolk?
> How long will the naive sisters be the targets
> of the fortune-teller's sorcery?
> O God! When will the girls read and write?
> O God! When will such a thing happen in Iran?
> How long will the superstitions of the preacher
> disrupt the people's pursuit of sustenance?
> How long, for the sake of a piece of bread,
> will a girl remain the captive of a culprit?
> How long will the prestige and chastity
> of the daughter of the poor remain a free commodity?[63]

Between the two world wars, the issue of women's emancipation became one of the most often discussed matters. 'Eshqi's "Black Shroud," Lahuti's "To the Daughter of Iran," and Parvin E'tesami's "Women in Iran" are only three of the poems written on the subject, but most such poems are not of a satirical nature. In Iraj Mirza, we find an outspoken poet

who treats the subject of women's emancipation in a beautifully vivid and spirited style combined with a far-reaching wit
and sense of satire. In one poem, he describes with great verve
how the ulema are horrified to see an unveiled female face
painted on the wall of a public bath and how they save Islam
from "shame" by fashioning a veil out of plaster for her!

On the portal of a caravansary
A fresco painting of a woman was on display.
The turbaned scholars heard the news
From a source trustworthy and true.
They exclaimed, "Woe to the faith!
Men have seen a female face unveiled."
Faith and peace were fleeing fast
Like lightning when the faithful arrived.
One fetched some soil and the other water;
They fashioned for her a veil of clay.
Chastity, which was going with the wind,
Was saved only with a handful of dust.
When the religion of the Prophet
Was out of danger, they went home and slept in peace.
Owing to this negligence of great magnitude
The savage folk were restive as roaring lions.
They would have torn the garb of chastity
Of that woman unveiled and open-faced.
Her lovely lips they would suck
Delightfully like sugar candies.
In short, the population of the whole city
Would be drowned in the sea of sin.
The gates to heaven would be closed;
Everyone would be packed to hell.

> This is why in the eyes of God and men
> So honored are the students of the faith.
> With scholars great as these
> Of the country's progress why should we despair?[64]

In his "Book of the Veil" (ca. 1294 Sh/1915), which was apparently very popular at the time, Iraj Mirza describes one of his youthful adventures with a beautiful half-veiled passerby. His first attempt at seducing her is unsuccessful; the lady becomes indignant at the suggestion that she remove her veil. In the course of a long and humorous discussion, the poet succeeds in his stratagem by strictly avoiding the subject of the veil:

> I opened my hand over that lovely one.
> As a molla on rice, a pious man on *helva*.
> But because chastity was in her face
> From beginning to the end she did not open her veil.
> Her two hands kept the veil taut,
> So that her chastity would not be lost.
> After I ate my fill of that sweet cake,
> She said, "May you choke on it!" and raced away.[65]

The difference between outward appearance and actual character is the focal point of Iraj Mirza's satire. The story describes the type of woman who dons the veil out of habit rather than from any consideration for chastity. A similar duality in action and belief can be seen in many female characters of modern Iranian novels and short stories. Sadeq Hedayat's novella *ʿAlawiya Khanom* is a graphic picture of the pilgrimage of a group of men, women, and children to the shrine of Imam Reza in Mashhad. Their characters and language as well as their

ignorance and degradation are depicted with consummate viv-
idness and skill. 'Alawiya Khanom, an outwardly pious but
inwardly vicious woman, is the dominant figure of the story.
She epitomizes hypocrisy and sanctimony.

Over the past few decades, there has been a marked
change in satirical works on women. Because there was no
need to make either the veil or women's superstitions the
subjects of criticism, Iranian writers gradually began to find
fault with new ways of life. The women who sought equality
with men in everything were often scoffed at as unfeminine,
and henpecked husbands became the pathetic heroes of many
comical short stories. Fashionable and extravagant wives who
ruin their husbands by slavishly following every new fashion
formed another category of satire. Gholam-Reza Ruhani (d.
1363 Sh/1985) was a poet and satirist who commented on
many social problems, among them extravagant wives:

> It is New Year's Eve and I am in a bad pickle with my wife;
>> Save me from my wife!
> She is my mate and I am a mate to sorrow and strife;
>> Save me from my wife!
> She wants a dress of Georgette crepe or jersey and voile
>> Of the latest style.
> But I have neither a pair of pants nor proper attire;
>> Save me from my wife!
> . . .
> Like an ass I am stuck in the mud, and my heart is full of
>> despair,
> She thinks of nothing but of coquetry and airs.
> She wants Coty perfume to buy for her hair,
>> O God, save me from my wife![66]

Because we have been considering antifeminist satire written by men, it is not inappropriate to comment on a few works by Iranian women answering such men. Bibi Khanom's *The Vices of Men,* whose translation we have offered in this book, is one of the first examples of such satire written by women. In her pungent satirical work, she answers *The Education of Women,* which was apparently written by a hotheaded Qajar prince who equated the pleasure of God with the pleasure of the husband and His wrath with that of the husband. Diligent and devoted service by the wife will be rewarded by her admission to heaven, whereas her wrath at the husband will be punished by the fire of hell. Bibi Khanom's answers to such absurdities are scathingly indignant. She writes that this genius of the world and unique writer of her times seems strangely bereft of his senses. "May it be that you are one of those devils, and with this device and deceit you have printed this book, making yourself their counselor so that they will end up in your trap. It is strange that this ignoramus, who considers himself one of those so-called westernized and civilized people and an imitator of European teachers, nevertheless clearly is not even half-civilized." Bibi Khanom points out that Iranian men say that "a woman has to take small steps and talk softly and weakly like a person who has just risen from the sickbed." Or they say, "She should not talk, make no sound, not answer anyone—meaning play pantomime— and eat with three fingers." But what if, she asks, "a woman with a few children sits like that at the tablecloth, would [her] children leave a single dish unturned, and would they give anyone occasion to eat? If a woman remains silent, those children will pour the bowl of sauce [*khoresh*] into the juice or the juice on top of the rice. . . . Yes, if a man with his wife, in the manner of Europeans, goes to a hotel, perhaps they can behave according to his instructions."

Bibi Khanom answers every argument raised by the writer of *The Education of Women,* often in the process engaging in humorous wordplay. She concludes that the work is a Fazihat-Nameh (Book of Malice) and says that such men as the author are not *rejal* (men) but rather *rajjal* (scoundrels). She ends her treatise with a poetic diatribe on such men and wishes that instead of expressing such high-flown ideas, they would spend some time serving their own people so as not to feel ashamed "before both men and God."

Another interesting writer of this period, who knew French and was familiar with European thought, is Taj al-Saltaneh (1263–1315 Sh/1884–1936), the daughter of Naser al-Din Shah. An amazing revolutionary in her ideas about social reform, Taj al-Saltaneh fought corruption and discrimination against women and was even critical of her father's shortcomings. Though the recently published autobiography of this enlightened princess is not satirical, it is a very valuable document on the emancipation of women in Iran. We read that the author had forsaken her old religious beliefs and was burning with the desire to go to Europe in order to meet "the women who had fought for their rights." She wanted to tell them that "when, overcome with happiness and dignity, you are fighting for your rights . . . cast a glance to Iran, where some creatures, wretched and broken, pale and sallow, some hungry and some naked, some crying day and night, but all in the chains of captivity" spend their lives. She says that Iranian women appear either in the "horrible" black veil of the funeral or the white winding sheets of death. "I am one of those unhappy women who prefers the white winding sheets to the terrifying funeral dress because compared to this life of darkness, death is our bright day."[67]

The Iranian poet Parvin E'tesami (d. 1320 Sh/1941)—reminiscing in 1934, when the veil was banned, on the past fate of Iranian women—echoed Taj al-Saltaneh: "No one like a woman did live in the dark for centuries; / No one like her was a sacrifice on the altar of hypocrisies."[68]

Nearer to our time, Forugh Farrokhzad (1313–45 Sh/ 1935–67) in numerous poems took up the cause of women and daringly and openly spoke about her innermost feelings of love and passion. She not only revolted against the destiny of women as dictated by men, but she also ridiculed the women who instead of being emancipated are lulled into inertia by their husbands' wealth and thus forget about their rights. In her poem entitled "My Heart Grieves for the Garden," she talks of her "sister" who in just this way has lost all her simplicity and naturalness:

> Her house is on the other side of town.
> And inside her artificial house
> with her artificial goldfish;
> in the shelter of the love of her artificial husband
> beneath the branches of her artificial apple trees;
> she sings her artificial songs
> and produces natural babies.
> Whenever she comes to see us
> and the poverty of the garden defiles
> the corners of her hem
> she takes a bath of eau-de-cologne
> Whenever she comes to see us
> She is pregnant.[69]

For Forugh Farrokhzad, such women, who are ready to trade human dignity and rights for the amenities of modern life, are "like zero in addition or subtraction [and] always end up with the same result."[70] In her poem "Mechanical Doll," she describes with amazing power and insight those women who marry out of necessity, not out of love:

> You can cry out
> in a voice utterly false and strange
> "I love—"
> You can, in the overpowering arms of a man,
> be a wholesome and beautiful female
> with a body like a chamois spread
> with large firm breasts
> You can, in the bed of a drunk, a vagrant, a fool
> defile the chastity of a love.
> . . .
> You can be like mechanical dolls
> and view your world with two glass eyes
> You can sleep in a cloth-lined box for years
> with a body stuffed with straw
> in the folds of net and spangles
> You can cry out and say for no reason at all
> with every lascivious squeeze of a hand:
> "Ah, how lucky I am."[71]

More than any other contemporary work, Farrokhzad's poetry represents the revolt of modern Iranian women against traditionally held masculine ideas and prejudices toward women. The shah granted Iranian women some rights, but these changes, like most of his reforms, were only cosmetic.

However, the passage of the Family Protection Law in 1967 was a significant step toward the improvement of the lot of Iranian women. Women were given the right to vote in 1963, but in a one-party system in which elections were often rigged, suffrage had little meaning. The political repression was so great that Iranian women took it for granted that their complete emancipation would come as the natural corollary of a change of regime. But with the upsurge of fundamentalism and the new brand of Islam existing today, they have been deprived of a significant number of rights that previously went uncontested. The family courts, which protected women's rights in marriage and divorce, were abolished immediately after the revolution of 1979, owing perhaps in part to the tremendous resistance to them by long-established patterns of male domination. In short, under the rule of the clergy it seems that Iranian women have been set back many decades. Further, if the present trend continues, the conflict between the sexes in Iran, far from being resolved, will become more intense than ever before.

NOTES

⸱※⸱

BIBLIOGRAPHY

Notes

Introduction

1. N. N., *Ta'dib al-Nesvan,* lithograph ed. (Tehran: n.p., 1304/ 1886–87).

2. G. Audibert, *La femme persane jugée et critiqué par un persan* (Paris: E. Leroux, 1889).

3. E. Powys Mathers, ed. and trans., *The Education of Women,* in *Eastern Love,* 3 vols. (London: John Rodker, 1927), 3:197–256.

4. Hasan Javadi, Manzheh Mar'ashi, and Simin Shakarlu, eds., *Ruyaru'i-ye zan va mard dar 'asr-e Qajar. Du resaleh: Ta'dib al-Nesvan va Ma'ayeb al-Rejal* (Bethesda, Md.: Jahan Book, 1371/1992).

5. Bibi Khanom Astarabadi, *Ma'ayeb al-Rejal: Dar pasokh beh Ta'dib al-Nesvan,* edited by Afsaneh Najmabadi (New York: Bloomington, 1381/ 1992).

6. Afsaneh Najmabadi, ed., *Bibi Khanom Astarabadi va Khanom Afzal Vaziri: Madar va dokhtari az pishgoman-e ma'aref va hoquq-e zanan* (Chicago: Midland Press, 1385/2006).

7. Bibi Khanom is borne out by the newspaper *Vaqaye-ye Ettefaqiyeh,* 13 Shavval 1273/6 June 1857, 4:2567, which mentions Mohammad Baqer Khan, son of the *ishik aghasi-bashi.* Mohammad Baqer Khan Anazani is mentioned again in April 1865 in the newspaper *Iran,* 9 Dhu'l-Qa`deh 1281/5 Apr. 1865, 755. He is also earlier mentioned in the same newspaper as chief of the cavalry *(sar kardeh-ye savareh)* of Anazan. See, for example, *Iran,* 11 Rabi' I 1280/26 Aug. 1863, 599.

8. For a description of Nowkandeh, a subdistrict of Anazan, see James Bailey Fraser, *Travels and Adventures in the Persian Provinces on the Southern Banks of the Caspian Sea. With an Appendix, Containing Short Notices on the Geology and Commerce of Persia* (London: Longman, Rees, Orme, Brown, and Green, 1826), 14–16, which reports that in 1822 Hamzeh Khan was its governor. In 1874, Rahim Khan b. Hamzeh Khan was its governor. G. C.

Napier, "Extracts from a Diary of a Tour in Khorassan, and Notes on the Eastern Alburz Tract," *Journal of the Royal Geographical Society* 46 (1876), 116.

9. Soheyla Torabi Farsani, ed., *Asnadi az Madares-e Dokhtaran az Mashruteh ta Pahlavi* (Tehran: Sazman-e Asnad-e Melli-ye Iran, 1378/1999), xiii–xiv. This book provides further information on how education for girls developed further between 1907 and 1925. There are two letters, very likely written by Bibi Khanom, addressed to the newspaper *Tamaddon,* 7 Rabi' I 1325/20 Apr. 1907 and 27 Rabi' I1325/10 May 1907; the former is signed by "Bibi," and the writer vehemently criticizes the reactionaries who are against girls' schools and says: "They know that if women are educated, men cannot dominate and tyrannize them." For other letters by Bibi Khanom and by her daughter Afzal, see Najmabadi, 59–97.

10. Farideh Mo'takef, "Madares va anjomanha-ye zanan dar dowran-e jonbesh-e mashrutiyat," *Rahavard* 85 (winter 1387/2009), 92.

11. We are grateful to Monica Witt for the tremendous help she gave us with translations.

Part One: *The Education of Women*

1. This poem is from the *ghazal*s of Sa'di, quoted in *Ganj-e Sokhan,* 7th ed., edited by Z. Safa (Tehran: Qognus, 1363/1984), 191. In citing specific editions of works in the notes to clarify the sources of unattributed verse in *The Education of Women* and *The Vices of Men,* our intent is merely to give readers a place to look if they wish to investigate further or read more work of the poets quoted. Following Iranian tradition, we are sometimes able to give only general information rather than citations to specific editions. If the reader knows the last word of a poem *(qafieh),* he or she can find the poem in any edition.

2. A wide mantle is the sign of a man who has achieved position and who is therefore presumably of a ripe age.

3. Koran 23:11 (al-Hajj).

4. See Sa'di, *Golestan,* edited by Gholam Hoseyn Yusofi (Tehran: Khvarazmi, 1381/2002), 100; this work has been translated into English as *The Gulistan or Rose Garden* by Edward Rehatsek (New York: Putnam's Sons, 1964).

5. This poem is by Farid al-Din 'Attar, according to 'Ali Akbar Dehkhoda, *Amthal va Hekam* (Tehran: Amir Kabir, 1377/1998).

6. These verses are from the *Mathnavi;* see Jalal al-Din Rumi, *The Mathnavi,* translated by Reynold Nicholson, E. J. W. Gibb Memorial Series (London: Biddles, 2001), vol. 1, lines 691–92.

7. It is said that Alexander, with the help of Aristotle, built a special mirror or reflecting surface in Alexandria in order to detect the approaching ships. It was called "the mirror of Alexander." Qalandars were members of a special order of Sufis who shaved their head and eyebrows. Hafez in this poem says: "A man with a flushed face is not a Qalandar. One who makes a mirror cannot master the art of Alexander."

8. This poem is by Hafez; see Hafez, *Divan-e Khvajeh Shams al-Din Mohammad Hafez Shirazi,* edited by Mohammad Qazvini and Qasem Ghani (Tehran: Zavvar, 1384/2005), 120.

9. See Hafez, 187.

10. Sa'di, *Bustan,* edited by Gholam Hoseyn Yusofi (Tehran: Khvarazmi, 1381/2002), 163.

11. See ibid., 108.

12. Imam 'Ali, *Nahj al-Balagha,* translated into English by Sayed Ali Reza as *Nahjul-Balagha: Sermons, Letters, and Sayings of Imam Ali* (Qom, Iran: Center of Islamic Studies, 1976), 224 (sermon no. 78) and into Persian as *Montakhabi az Nahj al-Balagheh* by Sayyed Ja'far Shahidi (Tehran: Elmi va Farhangi, 1368/2000), 58–59.

13. See Hafez, 85.

14. See Hafez, 96; *jam-e jam,* which we have translated here as the "Holy Grail," was the legendary mirror that allowed Jamshid, the legendary king of Iran, to see everything.

15. Foroughi Bastami quoted in 'Abdol-Rafi' Haqiqat, *Negin-e Sokhan* (Tehran: Elmi, 1350/1971), 6:591.

16. Sa'di, *Kolliyat,* edited by Mohammad 'Ali Foroughi (Tehran: Javidan, 2536/1977), Khavatim, 788.

17. Foroughi Bastami, *Ghazaliyat,* edited by Mansur Moshfeq (Tehran: n.p., 1336/1957), 235.

18. These lines are from a slightly different version of a poem by Sa'di, *Golestan,* 184. Hafez has a similar one; see Dehkhoda, 4:2034. Indigo was a color of mourning, and putting "an indigo mark on the face" meant to become a lover.

19. The text has a Turkish expression stating: "I am a man for myself, but you are also a man for yourself."

20. See Sa'di, *Kolliyat,* Forughi ed., 656.

21. See Hafez, 165.

22. This poem is by Sa'di according to Dehkhoda.

23. See Sa'di, *Golestan,* 123.

24. This poem is by Naser Khosrow according to Dehkhoda.

25. See Sa'di, *Golestan,* 180.

26. See Sa'di, *Bustan,* 163 (chap. 8).

27. Referring to Naser al-Din Shah (r. 1848–96).

28. This poem is indeed by Naser al-Din Shah; see Reza Qoli Khan Hedayat, *Majma' al-Fosaha* (Tehran: n.p., 1295/1876), 1:3.

29. Koran 21:18 (al-Anbiya).

30. See Sa'di, *Kolliyat,* Forughi ed., 553.

31. This poem is by Sa'di according to Dehkhoda.

32. See Sa'di, *Kolliyat,* Forughi ed., 355.

33. A steamboat was a marvel of rarity at the time.

34. This is a famous saying, and the part "Save us from hellfire" is taken from the Koran 3:201 (Al 'Omran).

35. Forughi Bastami, *Divan-e kamil-i Foraghi Bastami,* edited by Edward Browne and Husayn Nakha'i (Tehran: Amir Kabir, 1336/1957), 73.

36. This is a *ghazal* by Sa'di in a slightly different version; see Sa'di, *Kolliyat* (Tehran: Markazi, 'Elmi, and Khayyam, n.d.), Tayibat, 291–92.

37. From Nezami-ye Ganjavi, *Sharafnameh* (Tehran: n.p., 1316/1937), chap. 58.

38. A *korsi* is a heating device that consists of a low table with a brazier of coals underneath. The table is covered with blankets, and family members put as much of their body as possible, feet first, under the covers and tables so as to keep warm during winter.

39. These two lines are from two different poems by Sa'di; see *Golestan,* 120 and 56.

40. Rumi, *Mathnavi,* from the famous introduction or *Ney-nameh.* The translation is inspired by that of Sir William Jones in A. J. Arberry, ed., *Persian Poems* (London: J. M. Dent & Sons, 1954), 118.

41. A *farrash* is a servant, literally "one who spreads the carpet"; the *farrash* was also often used to carry out punishments.

42. Ayat al-Korsi is a verse of the Koran recited by Moslems when, for example, in danger or fear of misfortune; see Bess Allen Donaldson, *The Wild Rue: A Study of Muhammadan Magic and Folklore in Iran* (London: Luzac, 1938), 109, 112, 137, 175.

43. See Sa'di, *Bustan*, 306.

44. See Rumi, *Mathnavi*, edited by Reynold Nicholson (Tehran: Tus, 1375/1996), 1:58, line 939.

45. See Sa'di's *Hazaliyat*, in his *Kolliyat*, Forughi ed., 469.

46. This translation is by Mathers.

47. See Hafez, 102.

48. On this custom, see Donaldson, 20–22.

49. Sa'di, *Kolliyat*, Forughi ed., 656.

50. This poem is by Qa'ani, the poet laureate of Mohammad Shah. See Qa'ani, *Divan-e Qa'ani*, edited by M. J. Mahjub (Tehran: Amir Kabir, 1336/1957).

51. Dehkhoda quotes these lines under the entry "Ayimeh" in his Persian dictionary *Loghatnameh* without giving the name of the poet.

52. See Hafez, 136.

53. This *ghazal* is by Mirza Naser Tabib-e Esfahani, quoted in Saber Kermani, *Sima-ye Sho'ara* (Tehran: Eqbal, 1364/1985), 267.

54. See Hazef, 134.

55. See ibid., 102.

56. On sexual relations, see Willem Floor, *A Social History of Sexual Relations in Iran* (Washington, D.C.: MAGE, 2008).

57. Sa'di, *Kolliyat*, Forughi ed., Tayibat, 544.

58. This sentence in the Persian original does not make much sense and seems to be corrupted. Bibi Khatun Jan Qohpayeh, according to Mathers (256), was a proverbially ugly woman, which would suggest a slightly different translation. However, the qualifier "Jan" was often used for courtesans; hence, we have opted for the translation given in the text.

59. Sa'di, *Kolliyat*, Forughi ed., 553.

60. Ibid.

61. Ibid., Tayibat, 648.

62. Molla Ghaffar and Sheikh Musa were sorcerers of ancient legend; see Mathers, 256.

63. See Sa'di, *Golestan,* 151.

64. This poem is by Sa'di, *Kolliyat,* Forughi ed., 466.

Part Two: *The Vices of Men*

1. The reference here is to the war during Fath 'Ali Shah's reign, when one of his sons, Hasan 'Ali Mirza, Shoja' al-Saltaneh, defeated Fath Khan Barakzay in Khorasan in 1818.

2. The Goklen are a tribe in Astarabad Province and in Khvarezm, but here the name refers to their tribal area. Torshiz is a town in northern Khorasan.

3. The so-called vapor-water pipe enables people to inhale marijuana vapor containing tetrahydrocannabinol (THC) and other cannabinoids rather than marijuana smoke containing THC along with all sorts of particulate matter, tars, and some gaseous products of combustion.

4. "Hashish is thought so badly of in Persia that it is usually spoken of, even by those who use it, by some nickname, such as Aqa-yi-Seyyid ('Master Seyyid'), Tuti-i-asrar ('The Parrot of Mysteries'), or simply Asrar ('Mysteries'), the first two alluding to its green colour. One of the odes of Hafiz, beginning 'Alaya tuti-yi guya-yi asrar, Mabada khaliyat shakkar zi minkar' ('O Parrot, who discoursest of mysteries, may thy beak never want sugar!'), is addressed to the drug." Edward Granville Browne, *A Year Amongst the Persians: Impressions as to the Life, Character, & Thought of the People of Persia, Received during Twelve Months' Residence in That Country in the Year 1887–1888* (London: Adam and Charles Black, 1893), 569 n. 1.

5. On rowdies and debauchees (*lutis*) and other urban lowlifes, see Willem Floor, "Lutis," in *Encyclopedia Iranica,* available at http://www.iranica.com.

6. Koran 7:179 (A'raf).

7. Mirza Ebrahim Khan Khalvati of Mahallat was the son of Mirza Ahmad Mahallati, one of the poets of Naser al-Din Shah's court. For his life, see Mohammad Ebrahim Madayeh-negar, *Anjoman-e Naseri,* chap. 4, no. 5, which is published in his *Tadhkereh-ye Majdiyeh, Anjoman-e Naseri* (Tehran: n.p., 1303/1883), 96–101.

8. This couplet is by Sa'di, *Kolliyat,* Forughi ed., 451. At this point in the text, three poems are given that eulogize Naser al-Din Shah, Mozaffar

al-Din Mirza, and the grand vizier, which we have not translated because of their extreme verbosity.

9. Nezami-ye Ganjavi, *Makhzan al-Asrar,* edited by Vahid Dastgerdi (Tehran: Armaghan, 1312/1933), 7.

10. The words used are "dwellers of the throne, were it not for you," which refers to the tradition concerning the Prophet that "if it were not for you, we would not have created the firmament."

11. Rumi, *Mathnavi,* bk. 1, line 131.

12. See Sa'di, *The Gulistan,* introduction, Rehatsek trans.; Sa'di, *Kolliyat,* Forughi ed., 72.

13. Koran 4:34 (al-Nisa).

14. According to Koran 64:11–12, many men had reached stages of excellence. However, from among the women, no one had reached a stage of excellence except Maryam and 'Ayesha. Maryam is Mary, the mother of Jesus, and 'Ayesha is the Prophet Mohammad's youngest wife.

15. Fatimeh, who is also called "al-Zahra" (the Pure One), is the Prophet's daughter; her mother is Khadijeh, the Prophet's first wife.

16. Asiyeh is the wife of Pharaoh, the king of Egypt. She is alleged to have saved the life of Moses from Pharaoh.

17. Haman attempted to convince Ahasuerus to order the killing of Mordechai and all the Jews in Iran, and Queen Esther was able to prevent this massacre. See Esther 3:1–2.

18. Shimr b. Dhi'l-Jawshan was one of those who killed Imam Hoseyn at Karbala in 58/680.

19. Sinan b. Anas al-Nakha'i was one of those who killed Imam Hoseyn at Karbala in 58/680.

20. The first two lines are from Hafez, 132.

21. Naser Khosrow, *Divan, qasideh* no. 173; for a specific edition, see Naser Khosrow, *Divan,* edited by Hasan Taqizadeh (Tehran: Azadmehr, 1381/2002).

22. The phrase *soloq va sholoq* here should be read as *soloq soloq,* which, according to Dehkhoda's *Loghatnameh,* is the plural of *saliqeh* (good taste) in Persian slang.

23. The house of the famous Persian painter and prophet Mani (ca. 240 C.E.); also his book of drawings, which he showed to his followers as a work given to him by angels.

24. This Arabic saying has been versified by Jalal al-Mamalek Iraj Mirza, *Kolliyat*, edited by Mohammad Javad Mahjub (Tehran: Amir Kabir, 1964), 50: "In the garden of the world—women are like flowers / Like roses and nasturtiums are women."

25. Koran 21:67 (Anbiya) ("Curse be upon you and upon what you worship").

26. This is a play on a similar poem by Asadi Tusi, where he says: "The wound of a spear hurts more than those of words. / This one hurts the body, that one the soul." Dehkhoda, 2:899.

27. The poem is from Sa'di, who says: "My brother, this is an answer, not a quarrel. / If you throw a clod, you should expect a stone in return" (Dehkhoda). A different variant is given by Nezami in "Khosrow and Shirin" in his *Khamseh* (Tehran: n.p., 1336/1957), 158.

28. When Majnun came in the disguise of a beggar to Leyla's tent, she broke his beggar's bowl, which he interpreted as being a sign of her love for him.

29. This poem is from a *ghazal* by Hafez, 61.

30. This poem is by Jami (1817–98/1414–92); see 'Abdol-Rahman Jami, *Mathnavi-ye haftawrang* (Tehran: Ketabforushi Sa'di, 1337/1958), chap. 5, and Dehkhoda, 2:854. There is a sort of pun on the word *bakhsh*, which in the first hemistich means "share" or "part" and in the second hemistich is a contraction of *bakhshandeh*, used as part of the compound adjective *hasti bakhsh*, "capable of imparting existence."

31. These two couplets are from chapter 7 of Sa'di's *Bustan*, the first line from p. 168, and the second from p. 167. They make sense in the full poem, but when they are taken out of context, their meaning is rather obscure. Sa'di's meaning is that whatever you do, you are not free from criticism of ill wishers.

32. This is a variant of a poem by Sa'di, *Golestan*, 156. The English equivalent is, "Faults are thick where love is thin."

33. The original expression at the end of this sentence is "quz balay quz"—that is, "hump on top of another hump." This expression comes from the following anecdote. One night a humpback saw genii dancing in a bathhouse, and because it was on the occasion of a marriage ceremony, he joined in; the genii were so pleased about this that they took away his

hump. When his fortune became known the next day, another humpback, wanting to be rid of his own hump, went another night to the same bathhouse and started dancing amidst the genii, but without noticing that this time they were involved in a mourning ceremony. They were so enraged about the dancing that they gave this hunchback a second hump on top of the other that he already had.

34. See Sa'di's *Hazaliyat* in his *Kolliyat,* edited by 'Abbas Eqbal Ashtiyani (Tehran: Adab, 1317/1938), 395.

35. These lines are apparently a sample of a popular tongue-in-cheek song of this period. The first line of this song is also included in Valentin Alekseevich Zhukovski, *Ash'ar-e 'Amiyaneh-ye Iran (dar 'asr-e Qajar),* edited by 'Abdol-Hoseyn Nava'i (Tehran: Asatir, 1382/2003), 67, as the beginning line of another popular ditty of that period.

36. According to Dehkhoda, 1:65, this poem is from Rumi's *Mathnavi.*

37. See Sa'di, *Bustan,* 55, line 543.

38. Nezami-ye Ganjavi, *Makhzan al-Asrar,* 82.

39. The name "Abu Jahl" means "Father of Ignorance," and this person's real name was "'Amr ibn Hisham." "Abu Jahl" was the mock name given to him by the early Moslems. He was one of the leaders in Mecca before the city surrendered to the Prophet Mohammad's army.

40. *Chars* or *charas* is the resinous exudation collected from *Cannabis sativa,* or Indian hemp. The dried plants are shaken over a sheet, and a dust, or *gard,* falls on the sheet; this dust is collected and sold as *chars.* The dried leaves crushed into a powder make bhang.

41. Israfil is the archangel who will blow the trumpet from a holy rock in Jerusalem to announce the Day of Resurrection.

42. This line refers to the verse of the Koran (al-Nisa 3) asking men not to marry more than one wife if they fear not being fair to them: "If ye do not fear that ye shall be able to deal justly with the orphans, Marry women of your choice, Two or three or four; but if ye fear that ye shall not be able to deal justly (with them), then only one, or (a captive) that your right hand possesses, that will be more suitable, to prevent you from doing injustice."

43. This line is quoted by Dehkhoda in *Amthal ve Hekam* without the name of the poet.

44. This saying is from 'Obeyd-e Zakani's poem "Cat and Mice." For the full translated text, see 'Obeyd-e Zakani, *The Ethics of the Aristocrats*, translated by Hasan Javadi (Washington, D.C.: MAGE, 2007), 129.

45. *Teren*, from the French *train* and possibly short for the card game *chemin de fer*. *As* and *ganjafeh* are Iranian card games; see Willem Floor, *Games Persians Play: A History of Games and Pastimes in Iran from Hide-and-Seek to Hunting* (Washington, D.C.: MAGE, 2010).

46. Koran 5:90 (al-Ma'idah).

47. From Rumi's *Mathnavi*, Nicholson ed., bk. 1, line 71.

48. From Rumi's *Mathnavi*, quoted in Dehkhoda, 4:2028.

49. From Rumi's *Mathnavi*, quoted in Dehkhoda, 1:356.

50. See Hafez, 154.

51. This juice is called *shireh-e matbukh* and is a refined opium product made by boiling either raw opium or *sukteh* (see note 52) and collecting the residue.

52. Soot or *sukteh* is opium dross, the pyrolized opium residue that is scraped from opium pipes.

53. From 'Obeyd-e Zakani, "Cat and Mice."

54. Horr was one of the martyrs of the Karbala massacre in 680 C.E. and is especially venerated by the *luti*s (see note 55), whose greatest oath is "by the girdle of Horr."

55. The *mashti*s or *luti*s were Robin Hood–type bandits. They were members of the neighborhood *fotovvat* assocation, and they were not supposed to submit to anyone who did not abide by their code of *javanmardi* (manliness). They were variously referred to as *luti*, *dash*, and *mashti*, and, like the Khaksar dervishes with whom they were affiliated, they wore distinctive clothing but more stylishly. They had their own habitual café, or *patuq* for drinking, gambling, and other amusements. The best of this type of *luti*s were those who actually tried to live up to the ideal of the Robin Hood–type bandit—that is, to be a *javanmard*, meaning an exemplary chivalrous person in both spiritual and material matters. Because of their fighting skills and local connections, *luti*s were utilized by secular and religious leaders in their towns. In the nineteenth and twentieth centuries, these *luti*s were often referred to as "roughs" *(owbash)*, "knife-wielders" *(chaqu-keshan)*, or "thick-necks" *(gardan-e koloft)* and were used to organize "spontaneous" demonstrations.

56. Sa'di, *Bustan*, 157.

57. Shahr-e Now was the red-light district of Tehran from 1881 to 1979, and the women who ran the brothels there were called, among other things, *baji*.

58. A *maleki* shoe or slipper was a traditional cloth shoe; it consisted of a strong cloth sole and a cotton upper. The ones made in Shiraz were very popular.

59. Rumi, *Mathnavi*, Nicholson ed., bk. 6, line 290.

60. Koran 24:3 (al-Nur).

61. Koran 3:4 (al-Nisa). This line refers to the fact that in Islam a woman's "marriage portion" *(mahr)* should be paid whenever she wants it. The Koran states: "And give the women (on marriage) their dower as a free gift; but if they, of their own good pleasure, remit any part of it to you, Take it and enjoy it with right good cheer" (al-Nisa 4).

62. Koran 2:31 (al-Baqara). «If you divorce the woman, once they fulfill their waiting period, you shall allow them to live in the same house amicably or let them leave amicably. Do not force them to stay against their will as a revenge. Anyone who does this wrongs his own soul.»

63. This poem is by Vahshi Bafqi (d. 1583); see Kamal al-Din Vahshi Bafqi, *Kolliyat*, edited by Sayyed Ahmad et al. (Tehran: Sa'adat and Akhavan Ketabchi, 1347/1929), 362.

64. See Sa'di, *Bustan*, 168.

65. The blood price of a woman is half that of a man.

66. This poem was inspired by Sa'di's *Golestan*, first chapter, story 26.

67. This poem is by Mosaheb of Ganja, a seventeenth-century poet.

68. Koran 4:3 (al-Nisa): "If you deem it best for the orphans, you may marry their mothers—you may marry two, three, or four. If you fear lest you become unfair, then you shall be content with only one or with what you already have."

69. Koran 12:28 (Yusof).

70. "Farhad va Shirin," in Vahshi Bafqi, 388.

71. Koran 22:11 (al-Hajj).

72. Koran 14:46 (Ibrahim).

73. Koran 2:229 (al-Baqara).

74. Koran 2:233 (al-Baqara).

75. Koran 4:32 (al-Nisa).

76. This verse is from Nezami according to Dehkhoda 3:1397. In some sources, this poem is given as by Ferdowsi in the *Shah-Nameh,* but Dehkhoda gives it as by Nezami.

77. Koran 4:19 (al-Nisa).

78. This refers to the love of the Prophet Mohammad for his wife 'Ayesha, who had red hair and whom he called "my little red-haired one" (from Rumi, *Mathnavi,* Nicholson ed., bk. 1, line 2438).

79. Some consider this saying a tradition *(hadith),* and some a proverb. See Dehkhoda, 1:276.

80. See Rumi, *Mathnavi,* edited by Mohammad Este'lami (Tehran: Zavvar, 1874/1985), vol. 5, line 1595.

81. This poem is by the Saljuq poet 'Abdol-Vase' Jabali (d. 1160), *Divan-e 'Abdol-Vase' Jabali,* edited by Dhabihollah Safa (Tehran: Daneshgah, 1339/1960), 1:13. The Simorgh is the Persian version of the Phoenix, a bird that goes up in flames and then is reborn. Alchemy is the art of transmuting matter by separating its elements and then joining them again, just like the Simorgh.

82. In 1243/1828, the province of Qarabagh was conquered by Russia, and many Moslem families fled to Iran.

83. This poem is by Farid al-Din 'Attar, *Mantiq al-tayr,* edited by Mohammed Javad Mashqur (Tehran: n.p., 1341/1962), 89.

84. Sa'di, *Kolliyat,* Foroughi ed., 735.

85. Ibid., Khavatim in *Kolliyat,* 791.

86. Omran's son is Moses, who spoke with God. The son of Azar is Abraham, who, according to the tradition, passed through fire. See Dehkhoda's *Loghatnameh,* under "Tarekh."

87. On the institution of temporary marriage, see Floor *A Social History of Sexual Relations in Iran,* chap. 2.

88. Sa'di, *Golestan,* chap. 1, story 39.

89. Sa'di, *Bustan,* 107, with some variation.

90. The poem is from Sa'di's *Bustan* (180) and refers to Koran 34:10 (al-Saba): "And certainly We gave to Dawood excellence from Us: O mountains! Sing praises with him, and the birds; and We made the iron pliant to him."

91. Sa'di, *Kolliyat, ghazal* no. 226.

Part Three: Women in Persian Satire

1. Quoted in Matthew Hodgart, *Satire* (London: World Univ. Library, 1969), 79.

2. Quoted in Simone de Beauvoir, *Nature of the Second Sex,* translated by H. M. Parshley (London: New English Library, 1963) 13.

3. For instance, in Arabic the terms *watti, rafatha, hakka,* and *dahaja* mean "to make love," but they also respectively mean "to kick," "to swear," "to overcome" (or "to attack with a spear"), and "to drag someone on the ground."

4. J. A. Decourdemanche, *The Wiles of Women,* translated by S. F. Mills (London: George Routledge & Sons, 1928).

5. Zia al-Din Nakhshabi, *Tales of a Parrot,* translated by Mohammad Simsar (Graz, Austria: Cleveland Museum of Art, 1978). See also *Ten Viziers. The Bakhtyar Nama: A Persian Romance,* translated by Sir William Ouseley; edited with introduction and notes by W. A. Clouston (Larkhal, U.K.: W. Burns, 1883).

6. Quoted in Naser Takmil Homayun, "Barrasi Moqe'iyat-e Zan dar Tarikh-e Iran," *Farhang va Zendagi* (Tehran) 19–20 (winter 1354/1975), 25. All translations are mine unless otherwise indicated in the notes.

7. Quoted in ibid., 26.

8. Quoted in ibid.

9. Sa'id Nafisi, *Tarikh-e Ejtema'i-ye Iran* (Tehran: Mo'asseseh-ye Motale'at va Tahqiqat-e Ejtema'i, Tehran Univ. Publications, 1343/1964), 1:29.

10. Quoted in Sadeq Kia, "Sokhani dar bareh-ye Zan az Adabi-yat-e Pahlavi," *Majalleh-ye Daneshkadeh-ye Adabiyat-e Tehran* 5, no. 3 (1337/1958), 82.

11. L. J. Larcher, *La femme jugée par l'homme* (Paris: Gamier, 1858), 152–53.

12. See Zardusht ibn Bahram, *Arda Viraf Nameh,* translated by Fargard 'Afifi Rahim (Mashhad, Iran: Daneshgah-e Mashhad, 1342/1963), 21.

13. Ferdowsi, *Shah-Nameh,* edited by Mohammad Dabir Siyaqi (Tehran: Elmi, 1335/1956), 2:487.

14. Koran 4:34 (al-Nisa). Wife beating was widely practiced in Europe in the Middle Ages and even later. In England, it was legal until 1660. In France in 1334, a man who had killed his wife while beating her was acquitted on the grounds that he was performing his "husbandly duties." See Larcher, 219–22.

15. Sa'id Nafisi, ed., *Qabus Nameh* (Tehran: Forughi, 1937), 98.

16. See, for example, Naser al-Din Mohammad b. Mohammad Tusi, *Akhlaq-e Naseri*, edited by Vahid Damghani (Tehran: Ketabforushi-ye 'Elmiyeh-ye Eslamiyeh, 1331/1952), 257.

17. Jalal al-Din Mohammad ebn Asa'd Davani, *Akhlaq-e Jalali* (Lahore: n.p., n.d.), 216–17.

18. Mohammad Baqer Majlesi, *Hilyat al-Mutaqqin*, lithograph ed. (Tehran: n.p., 1316/1898), 58.

19. 'Obeyd-e Zakani, *Kolliyat*, edited by Parviz Atabaki (Tehran: Eqbal, 1343/1964), 207.

20. Abu Nasr 'Ali b. Ahmad Asadi Tusi, *Garshasb-nameh*, 2d ed., edited by Habib Yaghma'i (Tehran: Tahuri, 1354/1975), 35.

21. Mohammad 'Awfi, *Javame' al-Hekayat*, edited by Banu Mazaher-e Mossafa (Tehran: Bonyad-e Farhang-e Iran, 1353/1974), 663–64.

22. Ibid., 669–71.

23. Awhadi of Marageh, "Jam-e Jam," in *Divan-e Awhadi*, edited by Sa'id Nafisi (Tehran: Amir Kabir, 1340/1961), 548.

24. 'Awfi, 637.

25. A quotation from the Koran (79:24) where the Pharoah claims to be God.

26. Farid al-Din 'Attar, *Tadhkerat al-Awliya*, edited by Mohammad Este'lami (Tehran: Zavvar, 1346/1967), 84.

27. Sayings such as "Mulier est hominis confusio" (Woman is the trouble of man) or "Mulier est sterci saccum" (Woman is a sack of dung).

28. For instance, the story in Rumi's *The Mathnavi* (Nicholson trans., 4:3544–76) of a lewd woman who makes love with her lover in front of her husband is the same as story 9, day 7, of the *Decameron* and Chaucer's *The Merchant's Tale*. See also on the subject Petrus Alfonsi, *Disciplina clericalis*, translated by P. R. Quarrie (Berkeley and Los Angeles: Univ. of California Press, 1977), and W. A. Clouston, trans., *The Book of Sindbad* (Glasgow: n.p., 1884). For a look at satire in general in Persian literature,

see Hasan Javadi, *Satire in Persian Literature* (Cranbury, N.J.: Fairleigh Dickinson Univ. Press, 1985).

29. Not unlike what the Islamic government is doing in preventing women from going to football games.

30. Rumi, *The Mathnavi,* Nicholson trans., 4:1337–429.

31. Ibid., 4:2332–37.

32. The reference is to the Koran 36:64: "On this day we seal up mouths, and hands speak out and bear witness as to what they used to do."

33. Quoted by 'Abbas Eqbal, *Majmu'eh-ye Maqalat* (Tehran: Khayyam, 1351/1972), 457.

34. Quoted in A. J. Arberry, *Aspects of Islamic Civilization* (New York: A. S. Barnes, 1964), 338–39.

35. Two well-known tribal families.

36. Hind was the wife of Abu Sufyan. According to a vow that she had made, she took out the liver of Hamzeh, the Prophet's uncle, who had been killed in the battle, and ate it.

37. Qa'ani, 10–11.

38. 'Obeyd-e Zakani, *Kolliyat,* 207.

39. 'Obeyd-e Zakani, *Ethics of the Aristocrats,* 70–71.

40. See Omar Khayyam, *Ruba'iyat: The Quatrains of Omar Khayyam,* translated into English verse by E. H. Whinfield (London: Trübner, 1882), 20.

41. Quoted with some changes from Edward Granville Browne's *Literary History of Iran* (Cambridge, U.K.: Cambridge Univ. Press, 1953), 3:119.

42. Ibid.

43. 'Obeyd-e Zakani, *Kolliyat,* 168.

44. Sana'i, *Divan-e Hakim Sana'i,* edited by Mazaher Mosaffa (Tehran: Amir Kabir, 1336/1957), 61.

45. Ibid.

46. 'Obeyd-e Zakani, *Kolliyat,* 168.

47. 'Obeyd-e Zakani, *Ethics of the Aristocrats,* 17. See also Browne, *Literary History of Iran,* 3:60, 166.

48. Asaf, *Rostam al-Tavarikh,* edited by Mohammad Moshiri (Tehran: n.p., 1348/1969), 81–83.

49. James Atkinson, *The Customs and Manners of the Women of Persia* (London: Oriental Translation Fund of Great Britain, 1832). Though this book has a different title, it is a translation of the *Kulsum Nameh*.

50. Agha Jamal Khunsari's full name is Jamal al-Din Mohammad b. Hoseyn-e Khunsari. For an account of his life, see Browne, *Literary History of Iran*, 3:373.

51. Agha Jamal Khunsari, *Kolthum Naneh: 'Aqa'ed al-Nisa va Mir'at al-Bolaha,* edited by M. Katira'i (Tehran: Athar-e Iran, 1358/1970), 9.

52. Bijan Asadipur, ed., *Kolthum Naneh* (Tehran: Amir Kabir, 1976), 79–81.

53. Ibid., 93–94.

54. Ibid., 34.

55. Mehdi Malekzadeh, *Tarikh-e Mashrutiyat-e Iran* (Tehran: Ilmi, 1347/1948), 3:89.

56. Ahmad Kasravi, *Tarikh-e Mashruteh-ye Iran* (Tehran: Amir Kabir, 1340/1961), 416.

57. Quoted in Ehsan Tabataba'i, *Chanteh-ye Darvish* (Tehran: Ketab-forushi-ye Ateshkadeh, 1337/1958), 24.

58. 'Ali Akbar Saber, *Hop Hop Nameh* (Baku, Azerbaijan: Azar Nashr, 1962), 142–43.

59. Ibid., 227; see also Hasan Javadi, "'Ali Akbar Sabir," in *Encyclopedia Iranica,* available at http://www.iranica.com.

60. Saber, *Hop Hop Nameh*, 33–34.

61. Ibid., 181–84. This poem has been freely translated by Ashraf Gilani (Ashraf al-Din Hoseyni, a.k.a. Gilani/Nasim-e Shomal) in his *Bagh-Behesht* (Tehran: Kanun-e Ketab, n.d.) as "Complaints of an Illiterate Bride of Her Husband to Her Sister."

62. *Sur-e Esrafil* 1, nos. 27–29 (1907; reprint, Tehran: Rudaki, 1982), 225–26 and 233–34.

63. Quoted from Hadi Sultan-Qurae, "Modernity and Identity in Azeri Poetry: Mo'juz of Shabustar and the Iranian Constitutional Era," Ph.D. diss., Washington Univ., 1997, 80; see also Hasan Javadi, "Mowjez," in *Encyclopedia Iranica.*

64. Jalal al-Mamalek Iraj Mirza, *Divan-e Iraj Mirza,* edited by Mohammed Javed Mahjub (Tehran: Amir Kabir, 1342/1964), 172.

65. Ibid., 77–81.

66. Gholam-Reza Ruhani, *Kolliyat Ash'ar va Fokahiyat-e Ruhani* (Tehran: Ketabkhaneh-ye Sana'i, n.d.), 224–25.

67. Taj al-Saltaneh, *Khaterat-e Taj al-Saltaneh,* edited by Mansureh Ettehadiyeh and Sirus Sa'd-vandiyan (Tehran: Nashr-e Tarikh-e Iran, 1363/1984), 99. For a translation of his memoir, see Taj al-Saltaneh, *Crowning Anguish: Memoirs of a Persian Princess from the Harem to Modernity,* translated by Anna Vanzan and Amin Neshati (Washington, D.C.: MAGE, 1995).

68. Parvin E'tesami, *Divan-e Parvin E'tesami* (Tehran: Majles, 1331/1954), 117.

69. Forugh Farrokhzad, *Another Birth and Other Poems,* translated by Hasan Javadi and Susan Sallée (Washington, D.C.: MAGE, 2010), 151.

70. Ibid., 67.

71. Ibid., 65–67.

Bibliography

Alfonsi, Petrus. *Disciplina clericalis*. Translated by P. R. Quarrie. Berkeley and Los Angeles: Univ. of California Press, 1977.

'Ali, Imam. *Nahj al-Balagha*. Translated into English by Sayed Ali Reza as *Nahjul-Balagha: Sermons, Letters, and Sayings of Imam Ali*. Qom, Iran: Center of Islamic Studies, 1976. Translated into Persian as *Montakhabi az Nahj al-Balagheh* by Sayyed Ja'far Shahidi. Tehran: Elmi va Farhangi, 1368/2000.

Arberry, A. J. *Aspects of Islamic Civilization*. New York: A. S. Barnes, 1964.

————, ed. *Persian Poems*. London: J. M. Dent & Sons, 1954.

Asadipur, Bijan, ed. *Kolthum Naneh*. Tehran: Amir Kabir, 1976.

Asadi Tusi, Abu Nasr 'Ali b. Ahmad. *Garshasb-nameh*. 2d ed. Edited by Habib Yaghma'i. Tehran: Tahuri, 1354/1975.

Asaf. *Rostam al-Tavarikh*. Edited by Mohammad Moshiri. Tehran: n.p., 1348/1969.

Ashraf al-Din Hoseyni (a.k.a. Gilani/Nasim-e Shomal). *Bagh-Behesht*. Tehran: Kanun-e Ketab, n.d.

Astarabadi, Bibi Khanom. *Ma'ayeb al-Rejal: Dar pasokh beh Ta'dib al-Nesvan*. Edited by Afsaneh Najmabadi. New York: Bloomington, 1381/1992.

Atkinson, James. *The Customs and Manners of the Women of Persia*. London: Oriental Translation Fund of Great Britain, 1832.

'Attar, Farid al-Din. *Mantiq al-tayr*. Edited by Mohammed Javad Mashqur. Tehran: n.p., 1341/1962.

————. *Tadhkerat al-Awliya*. Edited by Mohammad Este'lami. Tehran: Zavvar, 1346/1967.

Audibert, G. *La femme persane jugée et critiqué par un persan.* Paris: E. Leroux, 1889.

'Awfi, Mohammad. *Javameʿ al-Hekayat.* Edited by Banu Mazaher-e Mossafa. Tehran: Bonyad-e Farhang-e Iran, 1353/1974.

Awhadi of Marageh. *Divan-e Awhadi.* Edited by Saʿid Nafisi. Tehran: Amir Kabir, 1340/1961.

Bahram, Zardusht. *Arda Viraf Nameh.* Translated by 'Afifi Rahim Fargard. Mashhad, Iran: Daneshgah-e Mashhad, 1342/1963.

Bastami, Forughi. *Divan-e kamil-i Forughi Bastami.* Edited by Hoseyn Nakha'i. Tehran: Amir Kabir, 1336/1957.

————. *Divan Ghazaliyat.* Edited by Mansur Moshfeq. Tehran: Safi Alishah, 1336/1957.

Beauvoir, Simone de. *Nature of the Second Sex.* Translated by H. M. Parshley. London: New English Library, 1963.

Browne, Edward Granville. *Literary History of Iran.* 4 vols. Cambridge, U.K.: Cambridge Univ. Press, 1953.

————. *A Year Amongst the Persians: Impressions as to the Life, Character, & Thought of the People of Persia, Received during Twelve Months' Residence in That Country in the Year 1887–1888.* London: Adam and Charles Black, 1893.

Clouston, W. A., trans. *The Book of Sindbad.* Glasgow: n.p., 1884.

Davani, Jalal al-Din Mohammad ebn Asaʿd. *Akhlaq-e Jalali.* Lahore, Pakistan: n.p., n.d.

Decourdemanche, J. A. *The Wiles of Women.* Translated by S. F. Mills. London: George Routledge & Sons, 1928.

Dehkhoda, 'Ali Akbar. *Amthal va Hekam.* 4 vols. Tehran: Amir Kabir, 1377/1998.

Donaldson, Bess Allen. *The Wild Rue: A Study of Muhammadan Magic and Folklore in Iran.* London: Luzac, 1938.

Eqbal, 'Abbas. *Majmuʿeh-ye Maqalat.* Tehran: Khayyam, 1351/1972.

E'tesami, Parvin. *Divan-e Parvin E'tesami.* Tehran: Majles, 1331/1954.

Farrokhzad, Forugh. *Another Birth and Other Poems.* Translated by Hasan Javadi and Susan Sallée. Washington, D.C.: MAGE, 2010.

Farsani, Soheyla Torabi, ed. *Asnadi az Madares-e Dokhtaran az Mashruteh ta Pahlavi.* Tehran: Sazman-e Asnad-e Melli-ye Iran, 1378/1999.

Ferdowsi. *Shah-Nameh.* 6 vols. Edited by Mohammad Dabir Siyaqi. Tehran: Elmi, 1335/1956.

Floor, Willem. *Games Persians Play: A History of Games and Pastimes in Iran from Hide-and-Seek to Hunting.* Washington, D.C.: MAGE, 2010.

———. "Lutis." In *Encyclopedia Iranica.* Available at http://www.iranica.com.

———. *A Social History of Sexual Relations in Iran.* Washington, D.C.: MAGE, 2008.

Fraser, James Baillie. *Travels and Adventures in the Persian Provinces on the Southern Banks of the Caspian Sea. With an Appendix, Containing Short Notices on the Geology and Commerce of Persia.* London: Longman, Rees, Orme, Brown, and Green, 1826.

Ganj-e Sokhan. 7th ed. Edited by Z. Safa. Tehran: Qognus, 1363/1984.

Hafez. *Divan-e Khvajeh Shams al-Din Mohammad Hafez Shirazi.* Edited by Mohammad Qazvini and Qasem Ghani. Tehran: Zavvar, 1384/2005.

Haqiqat, 'Abdol-Rafi'. *Negin-e Sokhan.* Tehran: Elmi, 1350/1971.

Hedayat, Reza Qoli Khan. *Majma' al-Fosaha.* 2 vols. Tehran: n.p., 1295/1876.

Hodgart, Matthew. *Satire.* London: World Univ. Library, 1969.

Homayun, Naser Takmil. "Barrasi Mowqe'iyat-e Zan dar Tarikh-e Iran." *Farhang va Zendagi* (Tehran) 19–20 (winter 1354/1975): 7–65.

Iraj Mirza, Jalal al-Mamalek. *Divan-e Iraj Mirza,* edited by Mohammed Javed Mahjub. Tehran: Amir Kabir, 1342/1964.

————. *Kolliyat.* Edited by Mohammad Javad Mahjub. Tehran: Amir Kabir, 1964.

Jabali, 'Abdol-Vase'. *Divan-e 'Abdol-Vase' Jabali.* Edited by Dhabi-hollah Safa. Tehran: Daneshgah, 1339/1960.

Jami, 'Abdol-Rahman. *Mathnavi-ye haftawrang.* Tehran: Ketab-forushi Sa'di, 1337/1958.

Javadi, Hasan. "'Ali Akbar Sabir." In *Encyclopedia Iranica.* Available at http://www.iranica.com.

————. "Mowjez." In *Encyclopedia Iranica.* Available at http://www.iranica.com.

————. *Satire in Persian Literature.* Cranbury, N.J.: Fairleigh Dickinson Univ. Press, 1985.

Javadi, Hasan, Mar'ash Manzheh, and Simin Shakarlu, eds. *Ruyaru'i-ye zan va mard dar 'asr-e Qajar. Du resaleh: Ta'dib al-Nesvan va Ma'ayeb al-Rejal.* Bethesda, Md.: Jahan Book, 1371/1992.

Kasravi, Ahmad. *Tarikh-e Mashruteh-ye Iran.* Tehran: Amir Kabir, 1340/1961.

Kermani, Saber. *Sima-ye Sho'ara.* Tehran: Eqbal, 1364/1985.

Khayyam, Omar. *Ruba'iyat: The Quatrains of Omar Khayyam.* Translated into English verse by E. H. Whinfield. London: Trübner, 1882.

Khosrow, Naser. *Divan.* Edited by Hasan Taqizadeh. Tehran: Aza-dmehr, 1381/2002.

Khunsari, Agha Jamal. *Kolthum Naneh: 'Aqa'ed al-Nisa va Mir'at al-Bolaha.* Edited by M. Katira'i. Tehran: Athar-e Iran, 1358/1970.

Kia, Sadeq. "Sokhani dar bareh-ye Zan az Adabiyat-e Pahlavi." *Majalleh-ye Daneshkadeh-ye Adabiyat-e Tehran* 5, no. 3 (1337/1958): 82–87.

Larcher, L. J. *La femme jugée par l'homme.* Paris: Gamier, 1858.

Madayeh-negar, Mohammad Ebrahim. *Tadhkereh-ye Majdiyeh, Anjoman-e Naseri.* Lithograph ed. Tehran: n.p., 1303/1883.

Majlesi, Mohammad Baqer. *Hilyat al-Mutaqqin*. Lithograph ed. Tehran: n.p., 1316/1898.

Malekzadeh, Mehdi. *Tarikh-e Mashrutiyat-e Iran*. 5 vols. Tehran: Ilmi, 1327/1948.

Mathers, E. Powys, ed. and trans. *The Education of Women*. In *Eastern Love*, 3:197–256. London: John Rodker, 1927.

Mazali. Azeri journal (Baku), 1914–15.

Molla Naser al-Din. Azeri journal (Tiblisi-Tabriz-Baku), 1906–32.

Mo'takef, Farideh. "Madares va anjomanha-ye zanan dar dowran-e jonbesh-e mashrutiyat." *Rahavard* 85 (winter 1387/2009): 88–99.

Nafisi, Sa'id, ed. *Qabus Nameh*. Tehran: Forughi, 1316/1937.

———. *Tarikh-e Ejtema'i-ye Iran*. Tehran: Mo'asseseh-ye Motale'at va Tahqiqat-e Ejtema'i, Tehran Univ. Publications, 1343/1964.

Najmabadi Afsaneh, ed. *Bibi Khanom Astarabadi va Khanom Afzal Vaziri: Madar va dokhtari az pishgoman-e ma'aref va hoquq-e zanan*. Chicago: Midland Press, 1385/2006.

Nakhshabi, Zia al-Din. *Tales of a Parrot*. Translated by Mohammad Simsar. Graz, Austria: Cleveland Museum of Art, 1978.

Napier, G. C. "Extracts from a Diary of a Tour in Khorassan, and Notes on the Eastern Alburz Tract." *Journal of the Royal Geographical Society* 46 (1876): 61–171.

Nezami-ye Ganjavi. *Khamseh*. Tehran: n.p., 1336/1957.

———. *Makhzan al-Asrar*. Edited by Vahid Dastgerdi. Tehran: Armaghan, 1312/1933.

———. *Sharafnameh*. Tehran: n.p., 1316/1937.

N. N. *Ta'dib al-Nesvan*. Lithograph ed. Tehran: n.p., 1304/1886–87.

'Obeyd-e Zakani. *The Ethics of the Aristocrats*. Translated by Hasan Javadi. Washington, D.C.: MAGE, 2007.

———. *Kolliyat*. Edited by Parviz Atabaki. Tehran: Eqbal, 1343/1964.

Qa'ani. *Divan-e Qa'ani*. Edited by M. J. Mahjub. Tehran: Amir Kabir, 1336/1957.

Ruhani, Gholam-Reza. *Kolliyat Ash'ar va Fokahiyat-e Ruhani*. Tehran: Ketabkhaneh-ye Sana'i, n.d.

Rumi, Jalal al-Din. *Mathnavi*. Edited by Mohammad Este'lami. Tehran: Zavvar, 1874/1985.

———. *Mathnavi*. 6 vols. Edited by Reynold Nicholson. Tehran: Tus, 1375/1996.

———. *The Mathnavi*. Translated by Reynold Nicholson. 6 vols. E. J. W. Gibb Memorial Series. London: Biddles, 2001.

Saber, 'Ali Akbar. *Hop Hop Nameh*. Baku, Azerbaijan: Azar Nashr, 1962.

Sa'di. *Bustan*. Edited by Gholam Hoseyn Yusofi. Tehran: Khvarazmi, 1381/2002.

———. *Golestan*. Edited by Gholam Hoseyn Yusofi. Tehran: Khvarazmi, 1381/2002.

———. *The Gulistan or Rose Garden*. Translated by Edward Rehatsek. New York: Putnam's Sons, 1964.

———. *Kolliyat*. Tehran: Markazi, 'Elmi, and Khayyam, n.d.

———. *Kolliyat*. Edited by 'Abbas Eqbal Ashtiyani. Adab: n.p., 1938.

———. *Kolliyat*. Edited by Mohammad 'Ali Forughi. Tehran: Javidan, 2536/1977.

Sana'i. *Divan-e Hakim Sana'i*. Edited by Mazaher Mosaffa. Tehran: Amir Kabir, 1336/1957.

Sultan-Qurae, Hadi. "Modernity and Identity in Azeri Poetry: Mo'juz of Shabustar and the Iranian Constitutional Era." Ph.D. diss., Washington Univ., 1997.

Sur-e Esrafil. Vol. 1, nos. 27–29 (1907). Reprint. Tehran: Rudaki, 1982.

Tabataba'i, Ehsan. *Chanteh-ye Darvish*. Tehran: Ketabforushi-ye Ateshkadeh, 1337/1958.

Taj al-Saltaneh. *Crowning Anguish: Memoirs of a Persian Princess from the Harem to Modernity*. Translated by Anna Vanzan and Amin Neshati. Washington, D.C.: MAGE, 1995.

————. *Khaterat-e Taj al-Saltaneh*. Edited by Mansureh Ettehadi-yeh and Sirus Sa'd-vandiyan. Tehran: Nashr-e Tarikh-e Iran, 1363/1984.

Ten Viziers. The Bakhtyar Nama: A Persian Romance. Translated from a manuscript text by Sir William Ouseley. Edited with an introduction and notes by W. A. Clouston. Larkhall, U.K.: W. Burns, 1883.

Tusi, Naser al-Din Mohammad b. Mohammad. *Akhlaq-e Naseri*. Edited by Vahid Damghani. Tehran: Ketabforushi-ye 'Elmiyeh-ye Eslamiyeh, 1331/1952.

Vahshi Bafqi, Kamal al-Din. *Kolliyat*. Edited by Sayyed Ahmad et al. Tehran: Sa'adat and Akhavan Ketabchi, 1347/1929.

Zhukovski, Valentin Alekseevich. *Ash'ar-e 'Amiyaneh-ye Iran (dar 'asr-e Qajar)*. Edited by 'Abdol-Hoseyn Nava'i. Tehran: Asatir, 1382/2003.